P9-EER-503

Here Is Your Hobby:
ARCHERY

ARCHERY is among the first four books in a series designed expressly for the young person experiencing the early enthusiasm for a new hobby. Beginner or yearling, the reader will find in ARCHERY the fascinating background and lore of the hobby, plus all information and instruction needed to get maximum satisfaction out of bow-and-arrow days.

Titles in the HERE IS YOUR HOBBY series are:

ARCHERY

CERAMICS

FISHING

STAMP COLLECTING

10214

HERE IS YOUR HOBBY:

Archery

by

BERNHARD A. ROTH

G. P. Putnam's Sons New York

Library of Congress Catalog Card Number: 62-14385

Manufactured in the United States of America
Published simultaneously in the Dominion of Canada
by Longmans Canada Limited, Toronto

CONTENTS

Here Is Your Hobby: ARCHERY

I

Song of the Arrow

Why Be an Archer?

Millions who now pursue the bow-and-arrow hobby — in practically every country on earth — could answer the question in just about as many different ways. To an archer, his favored pursuit is as *personal* as his preference for a beat-up pair of old shoes over all the new pairs in his closet. The bow in his hands spells happiness, freedom as an individual, romance — call it what you will; at any rate, it suits him just fine.

The physical sciences involved in bow shooting fascinate one of my archer friends. He is forever weighing, measuring and testing new tackle and materials — formulating his own techniques. He is as keen about the potential "thrust" of an untried bow as a space scientist is checking out a new rocket engine.

Another bowman in our crowd takes to the field looking strongly like old Robin Hood himself. An excellent leatherworking craftsman, his trappings are ornate with finely tooled designs. The rainbow hues of his hand-crested arrows would stand out amidst the brilliance of a medieval tournament. Indeed, he can

British Travel Association

Replica of a longbow with staghorn tips is drawn by a bowman of the Queen's Bodyguard in Scotland.

quote the history of the longbow all the way from Sherwood Forest to the present. Despite his fanciful regalia, he is a serious archer; practices long and intently; and is a fine shot.

In rural America, the track of the redman is still faintly visible. Tales heard and read of the Indian's prowess at stalking and bow-shooting game in our Berkshire foothills, I am certain, helped arouse my early archery interests. Later on, of course, I was also caught up in the magic web with good Robin, Little John, Friar Tuck and the rest.

In recent times, many a U.S.A. archer has joined the fraternity because of favorable, new hunting regulations. Laws in most states permit the bowman a better chance of bagging bear, deer, antelope and other large game. Special, and earlier, seasons "equalize" his chances with those of the gunner. Anglers, too, have been drawn to the bow, as state after state has legalized the shooting of carp, gar, frogs and so-called "coarse" fish.

Perhaps you're one of the many who have found that the bow and arrow leads you straight to the wide, open spaces where the wind blows free — a blessed contrast to crowded cities and annoying road traffic.

Whatever spurs you, it's a cinch you'll find kindred spirits in today's bright world of archery. And with today's superbows and arrows, you'll be the best-equipped archer of all time.

Get set for some potent surprises — in hair-splitting accuracy, walloping bow power and brand-new twists on an ancient sport.

II

The Bow Has Many Voices

You'll think twice, no doubt, before enlisting in the bowmen's army. And it's reasonable for you to inquire, "What's in this sport for *me?*" What's the personal reward for a pastime that is, stated simply, a matter of bending one stick in order to send another stick hurtling through the air?

Let's run through just a few angles of archery interest. Look closely, and see if your particular wants are answered.

Nowadays, a lot of folks are keen about keeping in good physical shape. Push-button living makes it harder to do. Then, look to the bow to help tune up your muscles and pare off flabbiness. Just merely drawing your bow during an ordinary 28-target field round gives you exercise equal to lifting a couple of tons of hefty weights. Walking from one target lane to another amounts to a half-day's hiking, and a heap more fun for the archer. His mind and reflexes are busy and constantly co-ordinated.

As to sharpening your eyesight in a practical manner, you'll find archery hard to beat. The flick of a deer's white tail in the slash pine, the tiny aiming spot on a target face, or a squirrel flattened quietly against a tree trunk are all fair samples of giving your vision a workout.

Let's suppose you have a terrific hankering for nature's great outdoors. Your bow will get you there. Hunting or just plain roving will take you as deep as you like into the inner sanctums of the wilderness. In the archer's observant manner of movement, you'll get to know every grassy swale, patch of woods, swamp, woodchuck hole, otter slide and a zillion other natural wonders, within your area of operation. You'll begin to really *see* the terrain spread out before you, where you only *looked* before.

Meanwhile, an odd thing will happen to you, something that happens to all habitual archers. You'll gaze upon each scene with a new purpose. The distance, for example, between you and that brush pile where a rabbit might pop out, becomes a matter of mental calculation. And, let's see, had you better kneel to shoot, to avoid clipping an overhanging branch? Which way is that wind blowing, in the event you need to allow for it in aiming? Whether the rabbit appears or not, you survey the country closely, from the bowman's point of view. Each turn in the trail is indelibly printed on your memory and retained.

Maybe you respond to novel, fresh activities and the constant impact of ingenious ideas. There, again, archery is for you. Improvements in equipment are developing constantly. Bows get better year by year, as advances press forward in ease of handling, accuracy, durability, range, and shooting comfort. Arrow design penetrates more and more truly into the category of finely guided missiles, as the science of selecting shaft material, fletching, nocking and arrowheads probes into new materials.

If you have an inventive instinct, you will want to take part in today's constant experimentation in search of better methods. Dynamic change is the keynote of the archer's world. You will be most welcome to try your luck at revolutionizing it by discovering a more positive way to aim the bow, guide an arrow, or otherwise open up a whole new avenue of archery excitement.

Bowmen continually seek to keep out of the rut. Seldom is

the dyed-in-the-wool archer completely satisfied with his tackle. Hawklike, he keeps an eye peeled for the slightest indication of a new trend in bow gear and tries it as soon as possible. In the same manner, he goes out of his way to find variety in shooting. There is actually wide variety already in the umpteen formalized systems of target and field-course competition. Yet, there is hardly a club that has not added something "different." Stay with the sport long enough and you'll inevitably wind up doing some strange and wondrous shooting, such as: targeting on kites dancing in mid-air; dispatching flaming arrows; aiming your bow from atop teetering logs, from horseback and from tipsy canoes.

Just when you decide you know all the angles, a new idea comes along. You might think you'll do all your bow bending by daylight, but you're mistaken. For instance, you can daub your target faces with "glow-paint" and shoot them at night aided by flashlights. It's been done; and so has archer raccoon hunting, which is another dark-of-the-moon pursuit.

If the spirit of competition means anything to you, let it expand in the archery field. The monthly club challenge round, complete with medals, trophies and other awards, is a dependable tradition among target- and field-archery enthusiasts. You can shoot your way upwards from there through interclub, district, state, regional and national tournaments. You can even set your sights on an international crown to be won at annual contests currently held in Europe. And for those who don't reach the championships in competition shooting, archery offers many other forms of recognizing shooting skill. Most archer organizations award pins, medals and insignia symbolizing achievements such as for big- and small-game kills, consistently high scores, and outstanding services in support of the sport itself.

Do you like to be with high-spirited, fun-loving people whose interests are similar to yours? The bow and arrow form a rallying point for folks of this type. Also, the old weapon has a magic way of making all of its devotees feel like "members of the gang." Wealth, social position, and professional standing all go by the board — they mean nothing in terms of a person's ability to

G. Smith

Arrows that emit a high-pitched whistling sound add zest to novelty shooting.

shoot. Each archer must bend to the same discipline of eternal, intelligent practice, no matter who he is. Perhaps this is why bowmen are among the friendliest, most helpful and good-natured companions to be found anywhere in the sporting field.

Archery attracts many an ardent do-it-yourself craftsman. You will quickly find why this is so. Nearly every session of concentrated shooting needs to be followed by minor repairs and maintenance. Feathers fly off arrows; points are lost; shafts get bent; arrows vanish; and so on. Archery "service stations" are, as yet, few and far between. So you are thrown upon your own devices. Most chores of tackle mending and upkeep are simple and not tedious. The hours spent in the home workshop or den are pleasant and provide yet another source of personal satisfaction.

If you have more than ordinary interest in archery-craft, you may well develop it into a source of income, even if only as a side line. In nearly every archer group, there are one or two folks who turn their hobby into a means of minor profit — through selling custom-tailored arrows, homemade bows, tooled leatherwork, hand-painted targets; or serving as agents for one or another of manufactured lines of equipment.

Should you get carried away with this type of enterprise, there are plenty of examples among today's big names in the archery industry indicating it is entirely possible to make the jump from archer-hobbyist to successful manufacturer. It should be noted, however, that all successes have been based on long experience, careful study of the archery market, and sound development of product. There is stiff competition for the archer's dollar.

Once you have "gotten your feet wet" in archery, there's strong likelihood you'll hit upon any number of facets that will keep you permanently fascinated. Photographing archery action, for instance, may become an obsession with you, as it is with many another shutterbug. Painting archery scenes may engage those with an artistic bent. For those who enjoy reading, there's a treasure trove of books that will enthrall you with the bowman's way of life.

Ever feel like giving the other fellow a helping hand? There's a crying need for archery instructors and demonstrators to guide novices toward safe, enjoyable and effective shooting. The public at large sadly lacks up-to-date archery advice. Meanwhile, Scout troops, schools, sportsmen's clubs and outdoor-minded groups throughout the land are also awaiting enlightened leadership to better appreciate the true potenial of the modern bow as a means of wholesome recreation. Maybe this is where you'll fit in.

Whatever aspect catches your fancy, there's a good chance archery needs you. You'll be welcomed with open arms!

III

Getting Your Bearings

When the archery bug bites hard, you'll want to do something about it. You may momentarily get the impression you're alone, that there isn't another bow enthusiast for a million miles around. Before you elect to throw in the sponge, give the bushes a thorough beating. Odds are all in your favor you'll flush a fellow archer into the open. Interrogate him thoroughly.

Essentially, you want to find out who the local bow shooters are, where their course or range is, how you can go about joining forces with them. As with any other sport, it's pretty unsatisfactory to play a lone hand. The encouragement, guidance and facilities found only with organized archer groups are vitally necessary for you to get off to a good start.

What might be called the "decoy method" is worth a try, especially if you already have equipment of sorts. It works like this: You set up a practice butt in your backyard or someplace in plain sight, and commence blasting away. The idea is to let all and sundry know your interest. This puts the grapevine com-

Bear Archery Co.

Chris Kroll exhibits huge carp he shot with bow and arrow in Michigan swampland.

munication system into operation. The word gets around that you're a "bo'n'arrer" nut. Sooner or later, your open exhibition may reach the attention of kindred spirits. It can almost be guaranteed that if there's an archery enthusiast anywhere in your neighborhood network, he won't be able to resist. One fine day, he'll saunter up to you, ask to look over your tackle, and admit, "Yeah, I do a little Sunday bow shooting, myself . . ." And there's your chance to get a foot in the door!

You may uncover yet another passport to the local archery brethren by haunting the sporting-goods shops. Find one that sells bow tackle and get some knowledgeable clerk to spill what he knows about nearby activities. Then, follow up on "leads" he may reveal.

There's a fair chance your school physical education director may know where the archers hang out. If you're already a gun hunter or an angler, you might well query your fellow sportsmen next time you meet them afield. These days, any one of them might be an archer in disguise. Again, if your hometown paper has an outdoor editor, it might pay off to give him a buzz.

Should you still find yourself drawing blanks, drop a line to your state game or conservation department, usually located at your state's capital city. These agencies maintain close relations with all sporting groups, including bow hunters, and almost certainly can provide you with the name and address of a club near your home.

Frequently, all kinds of archery interests (hunting, fishing, targets, field competition) are joined together in one large state association. News of mutual value is circulated through the as-

Tackle manufacturer Ben Pearson of Pine Bluff, Arkansas, brought down this New Mexico pronghorn antelope with an arrow through the heart at 25 yards.

Ben Pearson, Inc.

sociation's channels. This often includes an annual directory of the location and shooting calendars of all member groups. Therefore, individual membership in the association will be distinctly to your advantage. And you will certainly want to join a local club to gain shooting and social privileges.

In addition, you might well consider supporting one of the national federations of bowmen listed later on in this book. In several cases, you will receive a fine magazine giving you a broader outlook on archer doings around the world. At the same time, you will be helping archery's long, uphill fight to gain status as a sport for everybody.

Although bow sport is winning ground steadily, it has many a long mile to go. You need not step far out of your path to encounter profound ignorance and misunderstanding of both the lethal power and the vast recreational opportunities built into modern archery tackle.

For the aforesaid reasons, you are well advised *not* to confine your affiliations to archer groups only. Archers need to demonstrate their wares to nonarchers if the hobby is to grow. Therefore, bowmen can be most effective in also linking up with organized gunners, anglers, conservationists, campers, bird watchers and those of similar outdoor-minded interests. Mutual respect leads to greater co-operation and improved outdoor sport for all.

IV

Tackle Shopping

Selecting equipment for archery is a great deal like buying a suit of clothes. In both cases, getting the right fit is all-important.

At the tackle shop, just as at the clothier's, personal taste and the limitations of your wallet will also *not* be denied. The object, as always, is the best quality the budget will permit.

The big puzzler for the beginning archer is: What standards and specifications to look for? Information that follows will be helpful; but there never has been a novice yet who hasn't at least one last burning question before laying his money on the sales counter.

Here, then, are a few approaches to use in assuring yourself of getting the best mileage from your archery dollar:

Do some shooting first: Nothing will sharpen your appreciation of equipment potentials and values more than actual handling. Track down the experienced bowmen in your neighborhood and examine their tackle. Question them closely and observe their

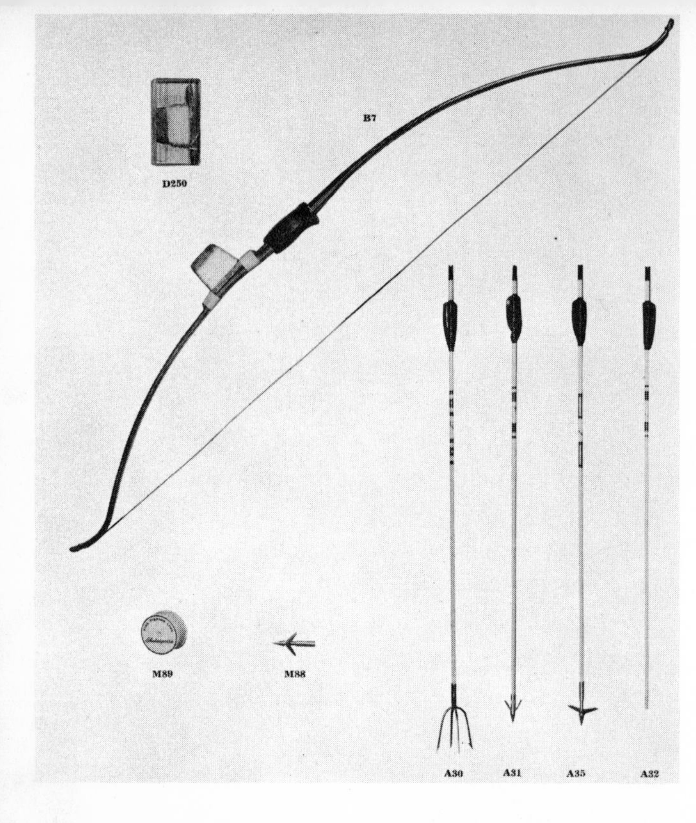

Shakespeare Co.

A factory-made bow-fishing rig with assorted rubber-fletched arrows. Shaft with fork-style head is especially adapted to frog shooting.

preferences. They are, to the last man, delighted to show their prized gear.

Get abreast of archery news: Interests and techniques are constantly changing and improving. Try to get a line on new angles by hobnobbing and talking with veterans "in the know." Also (we'll say it again and again) join a club at the earliest, to see, firsthand, which way the archer's wind is blowing. Subscribe to and read your state archery association newsletters, and the several good magazines now covering the field. By all means, take in target- and field-shooting tournaments and scrutinize what the advanced bowmen are using.

Study the market: Advertisements and sales literature are an education in themselves. Don't hestitate to send for and pore over a bale of catalogues to help you evaluate what's available, who's selling it, plus comparative features and prices. Hang on to informative material of this sort, as part of your archer's library.

Find a competent teacher: As in any other sport, a capable tutor can give priceless help to the budding bowman. While it's possible to arrange professional instruction, most beginners can locate more informal aid. A knowing salesman in an archery shop, or a friendly, experienced archer are likely candidates for the chore. Their mission is to steer you toward sound shooting methods and a happy choice of tackle. Final decisions are yours alone.

Don't go all overboard at once: Once the bug has bitten them, it is the impulse of all new archers to outfit themselves, in one spree, to the very eyeteeth, including those cute little Peter Pan hats with the gay cockades. Since, on today's market, this could easily tie up several hundred dollars, perhaps this word of caution

Archer specialty shops, when staffed with clerks who know the sport intimately, are well worth the beginner's investigation.

will be accepted. No one, at the very outset, has the foreknowledge to make so many choices wisely so soon. Happier will be the bowman who buys modestly, on a first-things-first basis, thereafter investing as he feels the need.

Who knows for certain whether his talents and instincts will lead him to become a dyed-in-the-wool targeteer, an upland field hunter, or a mixture of both? In whichever direction he is attracted, his equipment will need adjusting.

Buy from a qualified dealer: Thanks to recent efforts of the multimillion-dollar archery industry, this tip is becoming easier to follow. Yet one must still be wary of advice from sales clerks who can scarcely differentiate between bows and bean poles. (Not long ago, I saw one clerk attempting to brace a bow *backwards.* The customer left hurriedly when it broke in spectacular fashion.)

Be especially wary of "complete" archery kits packaged in the manner of children's toy sets. Many are excellent values, in themselves. But, in producing them for certain age groups and "average" physical measurements, manufacturers may be found to have fitted no individual shooter in other than a makeshift way. If you have no choice but to buy a kit package, open it and inspect it thoroughly to insure that the equipment is suited to your precise wants.

Archery enjoys many fine and reputable mail-order supply houses. Once a good one has been located and confidence established, this can be a satisfactory method of purchase. Some firms deliver with remarkable speed — shipping within a few hours of the order's receipt.

Visiting specialty shops when practical has many advantages. There is much stimulation in examining the wide range of tackle and accessories "in the flesh" and exchanging archers' gossip with men who know their business. An extra hour or two of travel spent on such a mission is a holiday well spent.

Should any real problem of finding equipment or negotiating with suppliers arise, drop a query to the Archery Manufacturers and Dealers Association. The address is AMADA, National Sporting Goods Association, 714 Rush Street, Chicago, Illinois.

V

Choosing Your Bow

Now, let's talk about the "engine" for your archery outfit. Putting romance aside for the moment, you will observe that the bow is precisely a mechanical device for delivering your arrows swiftly and surely to whatever target, near or far.

Maintain a cool, analytical point of view in picking out this power plant. It will likely be the biggest single item on your budget, and your companion for years. It will directly influence your success as a shooter. You will often think of the bow first in acquiring other parts of your gear.

Let's look at a bow — and *see* it, as though we'd never seen one before. Made of springy material, it has three main parts: (1) an upper limb; (2) a lower limb; and (3) a handle approximately in the middle where the limbs join. Great forces of *tension* are built up in the limbs as the bowman, drawing on the string and arrow, bends them backward. This tension is relieved explosively when the string is released. In *reaction,* then, the limbs snap violently back to their normal, braced position, causing the string to send the arrow on its way.

Hitt Archery Co.

Mr. and Mrs. Bud Hitt of Archbold, Ohio, developed tackle making from a hobby to achieve a nationwide reputation as makers of fine bows.

The prime mission of the bow, finally, is simply this: Each limb should be so perfectly tillered (balanced) as to deliver equal forces to the string at the exact point where the arrow is nocked. The resulting, singular force propels the missile in the flight path intended by the archer.

This brings to mind the most elementary first step in appraising any bow. Sight along its limbs both in repose and at the draw. Do they line up properly, twisting neither this way nor that? Or, in plain English, are they true, or just a wee bit cockeyed? In the latter case, you can well expect the arrow to fly cockeyed.

Actually, it's rare today that an improperly tillered bow gets past factory inspectors. For this, we modern archers can, to a large degree, give thanks for the advent of the *composite* bow. This design, too, like the familiar wooden variety, is actually a hand-me-down from history. Near-Eastern composites of animal horn and sinew were among the finest weapons ever developed. Rare was the bowyer who could fashion one; and princely the man who could own such a bow. That is, until today's era of fiber glass, micrometric laminating processes, and powerful new bonding agents.

The result is that mass manufacture of composites has added vast new realms of precision, quality and quantity. It has put fine bows within the reach of everybody.

Wooden manufacture requires the searching out of preferred species in the forest; selection of natural limbs or logs — free of knots, rot, cross grains or other defects; seasoning or kiln-drying the wood to a fixed moisture content; sawing out staves and blanks, or splicing staves together; then carefully shaping these, shaving by shaving, to proper tiller and form; and at length applying a finish for shipment to the customer.

Note this is a matter of building *down* from materials dependent upon nature. Composite manufacture operates in just the reverse. Here, the bowyer starts with a design based on the performance he has in view; then, using materials having known physical properties, he builds *up* to that design. This is not to say that composites are punched out like hubcaps for the family car. It is more accurate to say that the skills, arts and sciences (all are involved) of bowyering have swung to a different emphasis. They are now applied to a constant exploration of new formulas and blending of materials that climax in bows of splendidly engineered performance and beauty.

And where does this leave the would-be bow purchaser? The answer is it presents him with the widest, most dazzling assortment to choose from, in all the long history of archery. This can be confusing, particularly as a flowery touch begins to appear in advertising jargon. We can cut through the mystery, for the most part, with a short check list for you to run through in evaluating any bow on the market:

Draw weight	Handle riser
Draw length	Grip

Pull character	Bow length
Cast	Workmanship
Shape and design	Appearance
Shooting window	Price

Except for the *first two* items on the list above, and the *last,* there is no special significance to the *order* of their appearance. The first two features must surely match your natural physique and strength. While price — the final item — is forever breathing down our necks, it should not be allowed to becloud our ability to see a good dollar value. With that, let us apply the magnifying glass:

Draw weight and *draw length* must be considered together. Each shooter requires a certain arrow length, due to the length of his arms, breadth of his shoulders, his manner of shooting, etc. Therefore, the draw length of his bow must match. By the same token, each bowman is endowed with certain muscular power and this, too, the bow must match. Note that the strength needed to draw a given bow changes during the process of bending. So your objective is to find one that suits your power to bend it — to the exact point you will be drawing your arrow.

Do not feel you must put on the "strong man" act. Sure, you may be able to pull a 75-pound bow — once or twice. But how will your shoulders and biceps feel before you finish shooting 112 arrows in a 28-target field round? Nor do not, on the other hand, pick a weakling bow, either; or its short range and lobbing style of arrow flight may be disappointing. Best, for most beginners, is to choose a weapon that causes them just a little extended effort to bend. Almost certainly, their muscles will develop with regular practice.

Pull (or draw) *character* is vital. The best bows are engineered to provide the smoothest draw possible, all the way to full length of the arrow. Materials, shaping and other processing are tailored to relieve the "bunching up" *(stacking* is the archer's term) of resistance that occurs as the bow is bent. It spoils sharpshooting when the last few inches of the draw call for violent tightening of the muscles. Naturally, some build-up of tension will take place as even the finest weapon is drawn; but it should be subtle, easy-staged, in the one you accept as your own.

If you are a fisherman — and especially a fly-rod exponent — you will readily grasp the meaning of *cast* as applied to bows. It involves the efficiency and behavior of the instrument in propelling the missile. Amazing variations exist. Bows of quite similar draw weight and general design will yet have greatly different performance. For contrasting examples, one will shoot fast and silky, while another will be lumbering and slow. While speed in delivering an arrow is perhaps the prime concept of cast in bowmen's minds, a few extra refinements are desirable. Absence of shock or "jar" and "flutter," imparted to the bow arm by recoil, is a blessing.

Noisiness due to bow materials or design is understandably "poison" to the bow hunter. Fortunately, tackle makers can now take care of most of these problems. More and more of the brethren can truthfully say, "Man, I've got a sweet bow!" Translated roughly, this means the weapon has excellent pull character, plus cast that superbly suits the owner.

Turning now to the center section or *handle* portion of the bow, we find several practical ideas have recently been borrowed from firearms. Various types of *grips* are now available to match the individual's bow hand and shooting style. The recessed "pistol-grip," for example, suits the popular, straight-wrist method of holding the bow. An added thumb rest on some models gives further comfort and stability for better scores. Since the bracing point of the bow at draw is actually the palm of the hand, we suggest trying several grips in search of one that feels just right. You'll note that polished grip surfaces have largely taken the place of leather or fabric wrappings. This eliminates friction and the tendency of the bow hand to "lock" before the correct aiming position is reached.

Center-shot or semicenter-shot *shooting windows* — through which arrows pass — are now present on nearly all but utility-grade weapons. This is a contribution of modern composite bow-

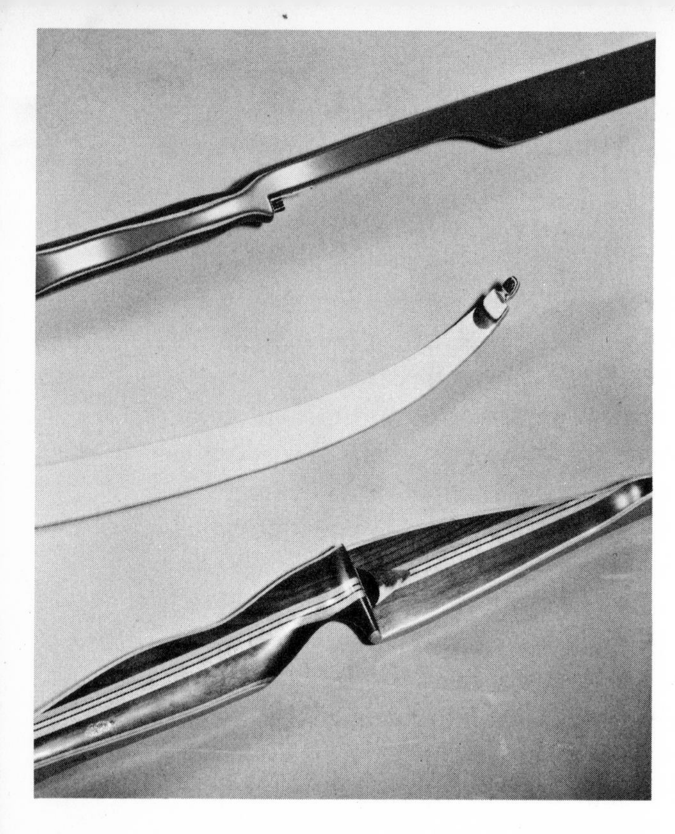

Shakespeare Co.

Close-up shows features of modern bow: *(top to bottom)* generous sighting window; reinforced bow tip; deep overdraw section with feather arrow rest and cowhide plate.

making. Solid wooden bows tend to be weakened by cutaways in the center section.

One can easily see the advantage of the window. Force of the string and direction of the arrow are, from the instant of release, more perfectly lined up with the bowman's aim. This reduces "archer's paradox." This phenomenon, seen in special high-speed movies, reveals that arrows actually wiggle, snakelike, several times on course to the target.

Main features of the window to examine are the *arrow rest* and the *arrow plate,* at the bottom and side, respectively. The best designs will offer a secure, ample channel for the arrow to travel through — at the same time causing the *least* amount of friction. Contouring of these surfaces is a help. So are rests and plates made of feathers, plastic and other materials. If other features satisfy you, it is always possible you can add these refinements yourself, using ready-made products on the market. One more point on windows: a *generous*-sized opening will aid in sighting the target.

You will find the newer bows are extra-thick through the mid-section, including the grip and window areas. The over-all effect is called the *riser*. This feature furnishes strength to the design and improves handling in the field. A riser of ample thickness is good insurance against "overdraw," the danger of absent-mindedly or excitedly pulling the bow back beyond arrow length. Results of overdraw can include shattering the arrow against the belly of the bow; or a painfully pierced hand, particularly where razor-edged hunting points are being used.

The *shape* and *design* of the modern bow have really gone wild. Most of the peculiarities are functional and are needed to give the performance intended by the bowyer. Others are frankly gauged to catch the eye and whet the imagination of the buyer, especially to remind him of archery's colorful legacy handed down from the ancient Turks, Persians, Romans, Crusaders, et al. Some of these flippancies do give zest and variety to the bow-shooting scene.

To grasp the rudiments of bow shape, let us take several of the more common designs, and hold each, in turn, in front of us, in the normal position of shooting. First and simplest of all (and doubtless the kind that is the ancestor of all others) is the *straight-limbed* bow, getting its curvature only when braced by the bowstring.

The next has straight limbs but, at rest, they bend *away* from us; this is the *reflex* design. Now here's one, also straight-limbed, but it, at rest, bends *toward* us; this is the *deflex* principle. Again, here's a design that first bends toward us, and then gracefully sweeps back and away from us; this is the *recurve*. Bows at your tackle store will be found to use the single or combination advantages of these basic designs.

Generally speaking, each built-in curvature aims to give the bow more "wallop" or otherwise improved cast. It is possible to be fooled by looks, however. Some beautiful bow curves do not necessarily contribute to shooting. Looking closely as you draw, you will note that the curved sections themselves may *not* bend, and do not therefore add forces to the recoil when the arrow is released. Top-flight bowyering, on the other hand, attempts to have every inch of the bow do a job. "Working" curves and recurves, etc., help fulfill that aim.

With the many avenues of design open to them through composite materials and space-age archery physics, bowmakers have considerable flexibility as to the *size* or *length* of models. Incidentally, the length of a bow is the distance from string-nock to string-nock along the back (the side farthest from the bowman) taken by tape measure. Whereas the "good yew longbow" of Sherwood fame was inclined to hover around six feet and better,

Five basic bow designs: (A) Straight limbs. (B) Deflexed. (C) Deflexed-reflexed. (D) Reflexed. (E) Straight with recurved ends.

Ben Pearson, Inc.

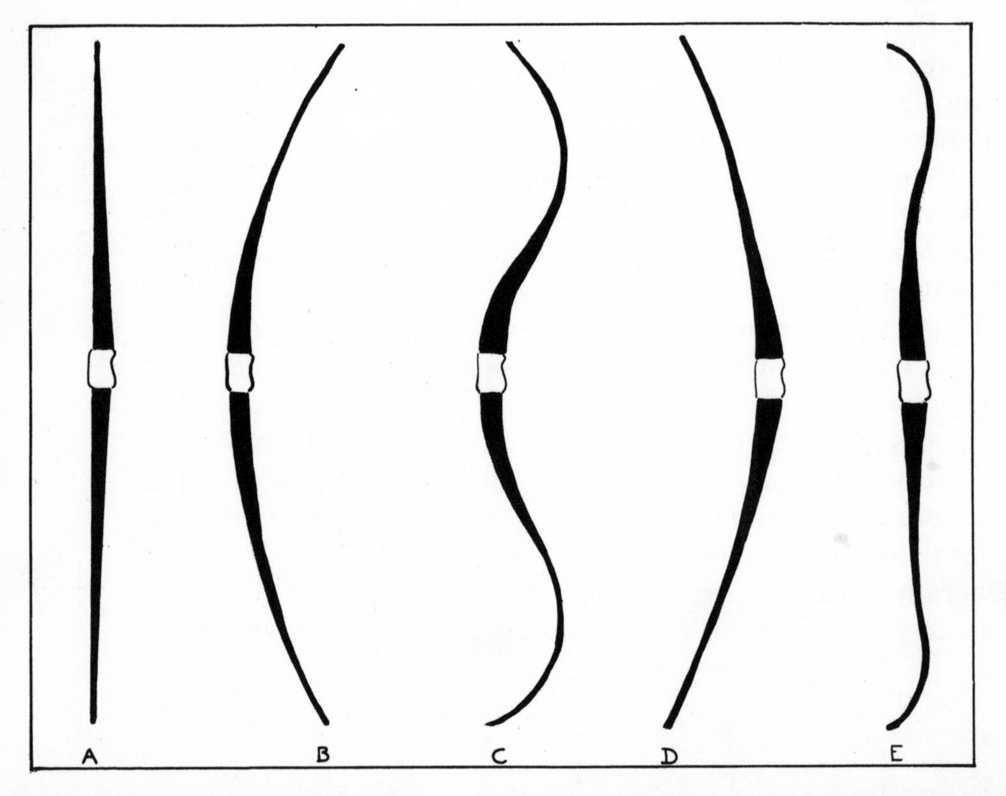

its modern descendant more nearly averages five feet. Designers can pack power into lengths shorter by a foot or so (such as for hunting, or for short, powerful archers); or may install the same drive in longer bows for individual taste or stature.

In a single design series made by one company, you can observe bows that increase in length according to the draw length required by the individual shooter. For instance, here are the specifications for a splendid line of sportsters currently on the market and available in draw weights up to 65 pounds:

Draw length	*Bow length*
29 inches	63 inches
31 inches	66 inches
33 inches	70 inches

Assessing the *workmanship* visible in a bow brings to bear just about the same standards applicable to any piece of hard goods. Are there flaws, cracks, chips, checkering etc. in the back and belly surface materials, edges and ends? Any evidence of poor or

Take-apart fiberglass bow is preferred by many archers who like compact, easily portable tackle.

G. Smith

lack of weatherproof finish? Are critical places reinforced? Is there built-in stupidity, such as nocks placed too close to the bow ends, or else so inadequate that each bracing of the bow is an exasperating experience?

Appearance is of course an accumulation of many visual factors of craftsmanship. Since there is no doubt that archery has eye appeal as well as numerous other attractions, it does no harm to purchase a bow also because of its beauty and elegance, if it is otherwise certain to give shooting satisfaction. More power to the idea! Bows in all or most colors of the rainbow, mottled and single toned, are now available. It is increasingly common to see incorporation of rare, exotic, handsomely finished woods and inlays of ivory and other decorations.

On the delicate subject of price, follow this tip from good old Will Shakespeare, "Costly thy habit as thy purse can bear . . ." which he goes on to qualify wisely. My own interpretation, right or wrong, is to get the best you can afford, being neither too much a piker, nor too much a big sport. Translated to bow buying, this means spending somewhere between $10 and $100 plus for your final selection. As in anything else, cost is a rough but not absolute guide to quality. For instance, not long ago we heard a veteran dealer say, "We offer one line costing over $100 apiece simply because we have customers who *insist* on spending over $100 for a bow and don't feel right unless they do."

To get some sort of index, a mixed group of 28 archers — men, women and teen-agers — were polled at a Sunday afternoon, club field shoot. Most were regulars admitting to exercising their skills steadily year-round on targets and hunting. The average cost of their bows came to just over $47.

VI

The Bow Bends a Long Way Back

Surely no one can shoot a bow regularly without sensing now and again a ghostly tap on the shoulder from some kindred bowman of the olden times.

Standing dimly at our side is that skin-clad, low-browed genius who never had a name. He bent a stick, braced it with a thong or perhaps a length of vine. Monkey-fashion, he fiddled with the gadget, finally poked another stick into it, snapped it, and was delighted to see the shaft fly away from him.

A brilliant light flashed in his untutored brain. This thing *might* shoot his spear. His big spear was too heavy. He made a little one, bent it into the gadget, released it, and the *first arrow* zipped off into the bushes, possibly shooting a sabre-toothed tiger lurking around for his hoped-for evening meal.

Where, on the face of the earth, did that first great experiment take place? Doubtless, as with most inventions, many men in many lands fiddled around with many little partial experiments before the bow and arrow emerged, full fledged. At any rate, the discovery is ranked equally with other sweeping steps forward in mankind's technical progress, such as developments of the wheel, lever, inclined plane, compass and the like.

Paintings and carvings on the walls of caves and on rocks in Spain, France and Sweden show the bow in use at least 50,000 years ago. Long before and ever since, the weapon has persisted in vital, everyday use somewhere on the planet. With remote primitive tribes of South America and Africa, it has remained at Stone Age level — a small, weak instrument suited only for shooting small game and birds. Sometimes it is fitted with poison-dipped arrows for larger mammals and tribal warfare.

Meanwhile, steady improvements in equipment gave archery increasing importance in European and Asiatic history. Emperor Genghis Khan ravaged nearly all the then-known world with his mounted Mongolian bowmen. The Turks terrorized their rivals with bows that could shoot arrows a quarter of a mile. Japanese became splendid archers and adapted archery to religion.

The bow rode high in the tides of invasion and counterinvasion that swept western Europe. First, with the wide-raiding tribes of early Germany, who had learned the weapon from Norsemen, and then with the Norman conquerors of England, the bow grew to be a fearsome weapon of war.

England, even as she hammered out a national character and sovereignty of her own, gave the longbow its everlasting fame. It is said that the Welsh, for centuries on the defensive in their mountain fastness, gave Britain the *truly long*, longbow. It soon supplanted the shorter weapon introduced by the Normans, then flourished gloriously in the golden age of Robin Hood.

With the longbow, and a rigid, national discipline of archery practice that affected all males from boyhood until past military age, British armies became the most feared in all Europe.

Taking just one example, we look at the scene at Crécy in France on August 26, 1346. The British under Edward III have about 20,000 men including 11,000 longbowmen. They face a French army twice as large, led by King Philip VI. The latter forces swarm with heavily armored knights on horseback, supported by hired crossbowmen from Italy. Late in the day, following a thundershower, the French attack. On command, the English bowmen shoot, in regulated volleys.

The front ranks shoot point blank; those in the rear lob arrows overhead. Horses scream, bolt, buck and scatter riderless, as the arrows take effect. Sixteen times the French charge, before midnight, only to go down in a bloody sea of disorganized men and horses. Meanwhile, the crossbowmen are picked off at long range, as they try to crank up their unwieldy weapons. Many cut their bowstrings and run.

Victory cost the English 50 men. The French lost over 1,500 knights killed, plus numerous other troops who were not counted, as was the custom of those days.

A few cannons, as well as the crossbows, were on the field at Crécy that long-ago day. Both eventually doomed the longbow's

British Information Services

Drawing of fifteenth-century English archers illustrates the ancient longbow and the sheaf of arrows knotted at the waist.

military might. The crossbow was never so accurate at long range, but it did not require the constant practice needed for excellence at the "goode yew stave." Meanwhile, firearms became increasingly deadly. Together, they finally sounded the death knell of the longbow, in spite of special laws and many gallant attempts to save it.

Toxophilus, a classic book full of sound archery advice, written by an English schoolmaster in 1545, came out of this last-ditch stand. It was sponsored by none other than King Henry VIII, who ardently loved the longbow and wanted it to live forever. Although the weapon fell into neglect for centuries, Old Henry has clearly gotten his wish. His favored book, prepared by Roger Ascham, furnishes precise instructions in the art of shooting, that have surely helped create a brilliant revival of the ancient sport.

Although various societies were set up in England and elsewhere to preserve the bow, and rules of formalized competition were established, the nearly total eclipse of archery lasted for 300 years. Its comeback in America is credited to the exploits of two Confederate army veterans, Will and Maurice Thompson. They retired to the Florida Everglades, became amazingly skillful at hunting with the bow, including the wing shooting of waterfowl, and wrote about their experiences with tremendous enthusiasm. Their stories, called *The Witchery of Archery,* started a new wildfire of interest in the bow.

The Thompson brothers spurred interest in the formation of archery clubs; and, in turn, organization of the National Archery Association. Since 1879, the NAA has grown steadily in membership dedicated to improving skills, techniques and tackle of longbow shooting at standard targets. In America, it has salvaged the weapon from the scrap heap of Old World history, advanced archery as a sport that may yet re-enter the international Olympics. Meanwhile, the NAA made target shooting a standard physical-education activity at most American secondary schools and colleges.

In the interim between the two World Wars, Saxton Pope, a California physician and surgeon, turned all sportsmen's eyes

G. Smith

"So long as the new moon returns, a beautiful, bent bow in the heavens, so long will the spirit of archery live on in the hearts of men." — Will Thompson in *The Witchery of Archery*.

once again toward the power of the bow as a game killer. Hunting in company with a fascinating, primitive Indian named Ishi, and a West Coast outdoorsman, Art Young, Dr. Pope demonstrated time and again: The smallest, largest, and cleverest animals in North America could be felled with well-placed arrows. Details were set down in his still-sparkling book, *Hunting with the Bow and Arrow* (G. P. Putnam's Sons).

Widespread bow-hunting interest quickly followed. To sharpen skills needed afield, an archer group at Redlands, California, set up a shooting course on rough terrain. It simulated actual hunting conditions, stressed shooters' abilities to gauge distances and maintain accuracy in ungainly situations. It was the forerunner of the modern field course and, as the idea caught on, led to formation of the National Field Archery Association, in 1939. The advent of fiber glass in bow manufacture spurred the new sport phase, making possible a superior hunting weapon with a flat, fast arrow trajectory.

Field-shooting competition gained by leaps and bounds after the Second World War, as archery tackle continued to improve, along with laws enabling archers to hunt. The NFAA has long since been endorsed by its parent body, the National Archery Association. Among the estimated more than 5,000,000 hobby archers in the U. S. A. and Canada there is today a considerable two-way overlap between target- and field-bowmen. Many find both phases of the sport afford satisfaction, good comradeship and keen training that an all-around archer needs.

And so, old ghosts, and some younger ones, are indeed at our side, as we draw the modern weapon to our jaw. We see them reflected in the instrument itself: Length approximating the yew stave pulled with such deadly effect by the peasant archer at Crécy; limbs of flat cross section developed largely by the American Indian; exotic curves and recurves from the Far East; and a composite lamination of several materials in manufacture that would be familiar to fierce cavalrymen from ancient Mongolia!

VII

Much Ado About Arrows

Consider the fast, hectic life of an arrow. It will travel through space at speeds in excess of 150 miles an hour. At discharge from the string, it must absorb a walloping force of anywhere up to 100 pounds or so, depending on your draw weight. Its flight ends with shocking abruptness, in a straw butt, in earth, against a stone, in the shoulder of a deer, on the thick skull of a woodchuck, in the tough trunk of a tree.

Anywhere in a flight, it may glance harshly off branches, shrubs, grasses, rocks; pass clean through a running game critter or a swimming carp. Yet, each time its owner demands that his arrow be found, retrieved from its place of lodgment, in good condition to be shot again.

Above all, the shooter expects each missile in his quiver to respond uniformly to his bidding and his bow — to fly straight and swift to the mark.

Many a beginner penalizes himself by thinking he can get by with a motley collection of shafts. The "arrow barrel" featured at

G. Smith

Spine tester in action. Weight suspended mid-shaft gives degree of bending as revealed by the indicator scale.

our own club range and others like it, is a case in point. In this keg, we toss all foundlings picked up here and there as we shoot around the field course. Owners can claim them anytime, no questions asked.

Rarely does one see a well-equipped, veteran archer pawing over the barrel's contents. It's not a matter of dignity, either. Rather, the keg contains, usually, the meanest samples of arrowsmithing, as indicated by random lengths, ragged fletching, crookedness, uneven diameters and similar excesses. No wonder novices lose them. Their flight behavior is hard to predict.

Remembering that archery is a game of uniformity — of transforming yourself and gear into a co-ordinated "shooting machine" — you are well advised to look at arrows in this light.

To appreciate this phase of tackle, we'll want to investigate the importance of length, diameter, spine, weight, shaft materials, fletching, nocks and points. It may encourage you to know that once you've made certain decisions, you won't have to run through a long check list to select your arrows. You'll know what you want the instant you see it.

Length of the arrow you need is governed by the distance from the back of the bow (the surface nearest the target) to the string, when you have pulled it to full draw. There are several formulas for getting this measure. None is more certain than drawing an overlong shaft in a light bow, to the position of release. Then have someone mark the full-draw location at the forward end (foot) of the shaft. Measure from the bottom of the nock to the aforesaid mark. This is the system most used by reputable tackle stores. Write the measurement indelibly in your memory, on the top of the workbench, or perhaps on your bow. State it in terms

G. Smith

Field bowman's "ammunition" includes *(left to right)* three types of broadhead, a metal blunt, and a nonskid field point.

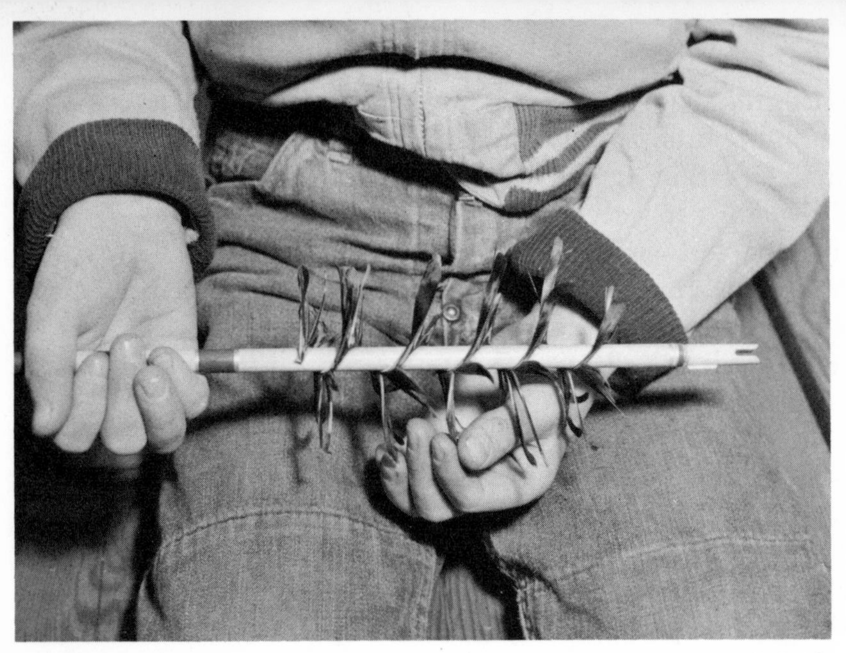

G. Smith

One style of flou-flou fletching is entire feather wound and glued around shaft. It "puts the brakes" on arrows, making them easier to retrieve.

of the nearest whole inch. Your physique and method of shooting are flexible enough to absorb any fractions involved.

You now have the basic length to specify when ordering. Target arrows with the familiar "bullet" point will thus draw practically flush with the back of the bow. Suppliers will automatically add length as befits other points that may be ordered. The length of broadhead arrows will be whatever is needed to prevent barbs from puncturing the bow or shooter's hand, at the full draw. Other hunting and hunting-practice arrows will match broadhead arrows in length as nearly as possible, so that aiming may be uniform in technique.

Spine refers to stiffness, or lack of it, in any given shaft. Technically, it is expressed as a measure of how much the shaft bends when a known weight is applied to it. Two prime factors govern the degree of spine required: one is the power (weight and cast) of your bow; the other is the length of the arrow. Simply stated — the greater the bow power, the greater will be the need for spine stiffness; the longer the arrow (with bow power constant), the more one must increase this same quality.

A heavy bow may send a soft-spined arrow wobbling all over the lot — or snap it, with hazard to the shooter. Yet the same heavy weapon may slam a too stiff shaft against the arrow plate. Having too little "give," the shaft will carom off course madly. With a light bow or a heavy one, the idea is to provide just so much arrow spine for shooting efficiency and safety without adding unnecessary weight to the missile.

Spine can be altered. In tubular aluminum or glass, spine can be changed by thinning or thickening the walls of the material without changing the outside diameter.

Since wood is a product of nature, its spine varies widely. For instance, one may test two dozen wood shafts of equal diameter to pick out a half-dozen matched in spine.

Should your arrows fly too sluggishly, you may want to experiment. Sacrifice a little spine in order to reduce weight and gain speed. Don't let yourself get hemmed in by "expert" theories. Archery is still a wide open game!

A brief word regarding arrow weight: It is commonly expressed in grains. One ounce equals 437.5 grains. Arrows average 300 grains for a target shaft, and up to 500 grains for a hunting broadhead. Shooting arrows of consistent weight is another aid to archery.

Now you have enough arrow background for understanding arrow-selection charts offered by many manufacturers. Running your finger down or across columns classifying your draw length and bow weight you quickly arrive at the other specifications. Diameters range up the spectrum from 1/4″ to 11/32″. Finer gradations (expressed in 1/1000ths of an inch) are available in the aluminum and glass shafts. Aluminum, for example, offers 22 different sizes including all the various combinations of diameter and wall thickness.

Some charts may give the impression that choosing your high-scoring set of arrows is a cut and dried affair. This is a false assumption. Sizes suggested by tables pertain to *average* bows.

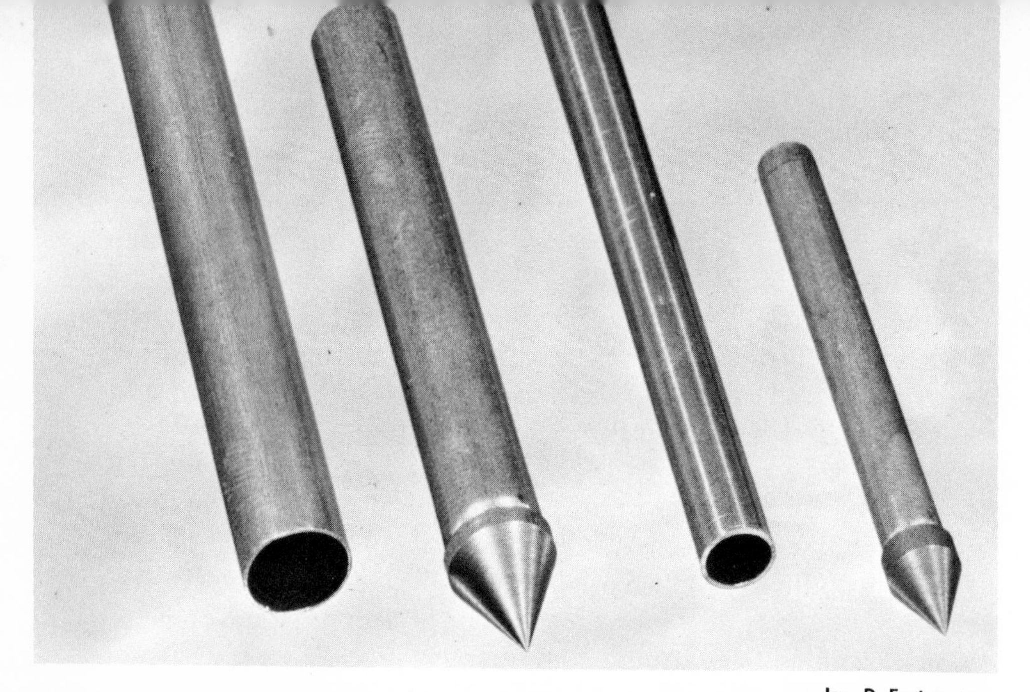

Jas. D. Easton, Inc.

Strong, durable aluminum shafts are available in 22 sizes, affording hair-splitting refinement of tackle.

They are based on scientific analyses and give priceless guidance. But they are not hide-bound *rules*. Each bow differs in cast, design, and degree of center shot; and so do you and I and the next archer as shooters. Thus, a single factor or a combination may change your arrow "specs," however slightly.

Some beginners may question ultrafussiness with arrows or other archery equipment. The record shows it does pay off. A stirring example occurred at the 1959 Ben Pearson Open Archery Tournament in Detroit. Jim Caspers of Racine, Wisconsin, brought the crowd to its feet as he calmly sank 89 out of 96 arrows into a three-inch bull's-eye from a distance of twenty yards. Jim's bow and shafts were matched to a cat's whisker in uniformity.

Should you become even moderately serious about competition shooting, you will study shaft materials. Wood is surely here to stay — especially the reliable, straight-grained Port Orford cedar. Durable, spine-and-weight-matched sets of finely finished shafts are likely to remain sound, economical investments for targeteers, field rangers and hunters, for years to come. Compressed, heat-treated cedar shafts with extra-tough footings are also a worthy refinement in wood.

Meanwhile, the advantages of aluminum and glass are now undisputed with a close race for popularity between the two engaging most of today's champions. Both materials are durable, weatherproof and precisely manufactured — and thus encourage precision shooting. Each will absorb great shock. Glass shafts, for instance, have been shot at right angles at a concrete wall without breaking. Striking hard objects at a more acute angle, glass may whiplash and shatter. In the same circumstance, aluminum will bend and need straightening, which requires a special do-it-yourself jig. An arrowsmith can straighten aluminum shafts for a few cents each.

There is one striking advantage to tubular material in the matter of maintaining *points* on the shafts. Note these are *inserted* in aluminum and glass, creating — with the newer gluing agents — an extremely solid, clean fit. They usually stay on

Die-cut plastic fletching in 4-vane arrangement cuts down air resistance to arrow flight; increases accuracy.

G. Smith

through all kinds of pounding until shafts themselves are destroyed.

By contrast, points for wooden shafts are glued on *over* the shaft end, which may have been tapered or simply squared off — depending on the bore of the point. Thus, the overhanging shoulder of the point tends to snag on target butts, making it more difficult to withdraw the arrow; this gradually loosens the point as well. I hope this does not sound like a terribly serious problem. It is, however, one that field and hunt shooters run into oftener than targeteers on their grassy plains. For instance, a practice range usually has a hard-packed excelsior butt that is death to all wooden arrows; it "chews off" points like a fearsome monster. Only the heads of metal- or glass-shafted arrows can escape its clutching excelsior.

Heads (or points — take your choice of words) are available for every purpose, be it competition, hunting, fishing, utility, or novelty shooting. Target points are traditionally bullet-nosed, light (about 35 grains), serving mainly to provide weight balance and at the same time protect the foot of the shaft piercing the target. Those that are "crimped on" wooden shafts by factory processes invariably are weak in the footing and break off early in life.

If the target shooter envisages woods roving too, it's a good idea for him to select all his points accordingly. Procure various kinds of points in identical weights, to avoid radically changing aim and style for each phase of the sport. This could mean, say, a 125-grain point in heavyweight target, blunt, field and broadhead forms.

Interchangeable heads are a fairly recent innovation. By means of a threaded ferrule attachment, blunts, field points, and broadheads may be screwed on and off as suits the emergency.

Blunts have a place in small game hunting. In shooting at squirrels, for example, one hopes the blunt will come bouncing down out of the tree, rather than stick up there, tantalizingly out of reach. One archer may always use blunts when shooting the field range, because they withdraw more easily from the butt —

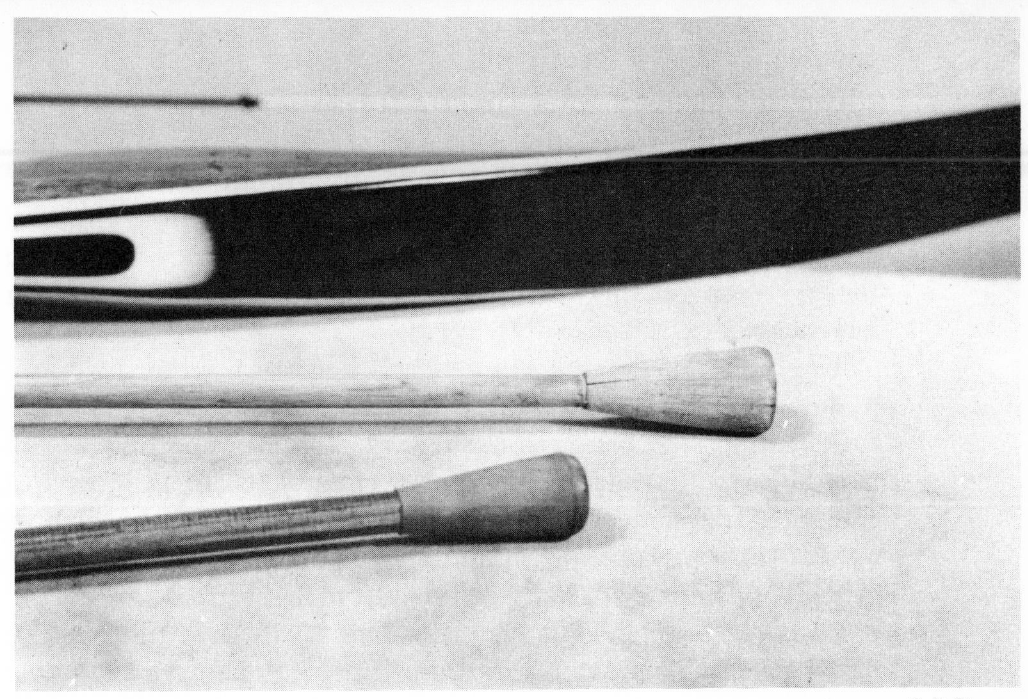

E. DeRienze

Blunts for small game hunting include rubber and plastic materials pictured here.

do not penetrate deeply. Another archer may prefer the nonskid variety. Blunts go skidding. Whereas, nonskids bring an arrow to a definite halt. Of course, the nonskid shooter should carry a pair of pliers to pry his arrows out of tree trunks.

The choice of points is wide among hunting broadheads. One finds 2-, 3-, 4- and even 6-blade models. Multiple edges face up to the sober fact that more game animals are arrow-killed by bleeding than by massive shock, which is the effect of rifle bullets or shotgun pellets. Exponents of the higher number of blades plead logically enough that the more cutting edges the greater will be the hemorrhaging. Those clinging to the traditional 2-blade design claim better penetration and thus an improved chance of piercing a vital organ.

You cannot afford to be overdelicate in this matter. If you elect to kill game, choose heads of maximum sharpness, of metals that will maintain a keen edge and can be honed to fatal effectiveness.

Broadheads, with their greater surface area, run into greater wind resistance than other types of arrows. To counteract their tendency to "plane" (in the manner of aircraft) or to be blown off course, heavier fletching is required. In comparison, the vanes of a hunting arrow may be as much as three times longer than those on a target shaft — up to 5 1/2 inches as contrasted to 2 or 3 inches.

The object of fletching in general then is to aid straight, true flying. Present-day fletching materials offer an option between turkey-wing feathers or thin, sheet plastic. Still another choice is whether to adopt 3-, 4- or 6-vane styling. The object in each instance is the same: improved stability in flight. Although the 3-vane style remains most popular, multi-vane styles are gaining ground and can be specially ordered from most arrowsmiths.

Enthusiasts for plastic claim it is more effective than feathering. They say plastic has less drag through the air, and otherwise lends itself to more precise fletching. The record shows it has scored well in long-range events such as flight shooting for maximum distance and the clout. In a clout shoot, a target flat on the ground is shot at from as far away as 180 yards.

For best results with plastic fletching, a special "shelf" should be affixed to the bow. Its purpose is to keep the extra-stiff vanes from whacking the bow in passage, which in turn throws the arrow wide of its intended path.

Spiral fletching — mounting vanes helically to impart a spin — is the common method, no matter what the material. Flight shooters, however, prefer straight (no spin) fletching in order to reduce drag. For bow fishing there is a real question as to whether any fletching is needed at all. It is doubtful if the vanes stabilize flight over extremely short range.

As to locating the fletching on the shaft, the determining factor is the clearance needed for the fingers when the arrow is released. Therefore, vanes should be placed at least an inch away from the nock.

Nocks of plastic are now in universal use. They afford smooth release and are tough enough to survive hard usage. Most are the "speed" nock variety, meaning that a slight ridge is found nearest the cock feather. Thus, by "feel" alone (without looking), you can string an arrow quickly.

With nocks of various hues, fletching in numerous colors, plus individual cresting, the archer can achieve a practical kind of gaiety in his arrows. Color serves at least two ends. It helps identify your arrows when shooting in a squad. Bright colors are more easily spotted in the inevitable search for strays. Still a third purpose is served by having a contrasting-colored cock feather; a mere glance then reveals the correct nocking position.

Finally, arrows are the "busiest" items in your archery gear, deserving far more than a passing thought. In fact, you find arrows remorselessly claiming more of your archery time — selecting, shooting, chasing, mending, etc. — than any of the other component hardwares. They are, after all, the means of expressing

G. Smith

Cedar shaft being checked to insure uniform weight in a set of homemade arrows. Hunting and field arrows average 300-400 grains — somewhat less than one ounce.

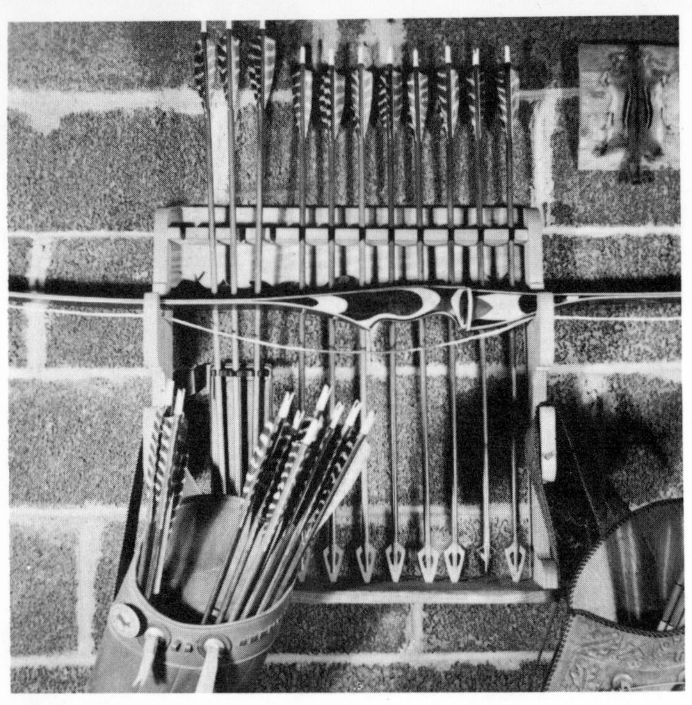

E. DeRienze

Protection for bow and arrows plus attractive wall display are embodied in this homemade rack for hunting gear.

your accuracy or shortcomings. They bring home the bacon — or else.

Will you ever own a *perfect* set of arrows? The answer is — no, but, for a price five or six times that of "expendable" shafts, you can have a set as nigh-perfect as modern manufacture allows. Even these will betray minor deviations in flight. You will mark each shaft according to its apparent habits, and aim accordingly, as the champions do. All of which brings to mind the old proverb, applying to archery as well as other endeavors: The real fun is in the chase, *not* in having arrived.

VIII

Get in There and Shoot!

As soon as possible after your enthusiasm for the bow has reached a boiling point, head for the shooting line. Studying tips on how to shoot beforehand will be of some help. But practice, practice and practice again will make you the sharpshooter you hope to be. Make it intelligent exercise wherein you constantly analyze your mistakes and rid yourself of them, one by one. For this purpose, there is no better aid than having a veteran bowman at your side. Persuade one to watch you closely, singling out and correcting your flaws.

For your initial training, we suggest a short range, say fifteen yards, with a 16-inch target and a 3-inch bull's-eye. This gives you a close-up view of your mark. Your wild shots will not look so discouragingly wide as they might at a longer range. Your morale will remain keen!

Let the expert loose a few shots while you observe. You'll note his movements are alert, yet unhurried and relaxed. There is no waste motion:

He looks casually at the target as he takes his stance, body erect, feet set apart, the shoulder of his bow arm directed toward the mark. Now he takes an arrow between his thumb and forefinger, meanwhile raising his bow in front of him until it is nigh parallel with the ground. He glances at his bowstring as he slips the arrow on the nocking point. The forefinger of his bow hand steadies the arrow as the archer dips his hand beneath the string, taking a 3-fingered grasp, bracketing the nock.

Now he turns his head deliberately and glares at the bull's-eye. Continuing to glare and without blinking, the archer brings his weapon up, around and forward in a revolving arc, his arms moving in co-ordination. Just short of the vertical, the revolving of the bow comes to a halt. The bow arm is extended with a firm, slight crook; the wrist becomes straight from forearm through the hand. Aiming begins as the bowman draws steadily downward on the mark. The arrow arm comes firmly, precisely backward, like the piston rod of an engine; then it, too, locks, the forearm high and secure. Fingers embracing the arrow nock and string are anchored, viselike and unmoving.

Suspenseful moments follow as the bowman seems to turn to stone; although close scrutiny reveals ever-so-slight movement of the bow as he pinpoints his aim. He freezes. Then, faster than the eye can follow, the draw hold relaxes, fingers straighten and the string surges forward. Twang! *Z-z-z-zip! Splut!* And there is the arrow buried up to its feathers in the bull's-eye!

Glancing back to the bowman, you note he is still standing like a statue several seconds after releasing the arrow, staring thoughtfully at his shot. His bow hangs lifeless in his extended grasp. His now-relaxed draw hand remains poised near the high-release position. But, already he is estimating how his next shot can be improved.

As you set out to follow the example of a good marksman, bear in mind that no two people shoot the bow in exactly the same manner. Differences in physical build, muscles, eyesight, co-ordination, habits of movement — as well as variations in individual equipment — account for differences in technique.

G. Smith

Left: Instep method of bracing the bow is suitable to most archers. Face should be held aside for safety. *Right:* Step-through method of bracing affords more leverage — may be needed for heavier or longer bows. Care should be exerted not to twist the limbs.

And yet, it is clear that all who become efficient with the bow do follow several tried-and-true basic *principles*. Chief among these is to become, as nearly as possible, a "thinking robot" while shooting. This means having a deliberate plan for all actions, however trivial they may seem, and performing them mechanically, time after time, in identical fashion. In this way, you can put your finger quickly on your errors, in order to toss them overboard.

Technique is made up of many, many little physical actions. They fall readily into a number of unified steps. Let's scrutinize them as though they were unfolding in slow motion. (Actually, the whole process can be accomplished at blinding speed. For example, one of my friends likes to challenge shotgunners. He invariably beats them by nocking and getting off an accurate arrow, before they can load and fire their weapons.)

Shooting stance: Of course, bow hunters must often shoot from whatever awkward position they can manage. However, be it paper target or wild game, the ideal remains the same. An imaginary line drawn through the shoulders or feet, placed correctly, would, if extended, pass somewhere through the target area.

Nocking the arrow: There are methods other than the one described earlier. One that supposedly came out of the Middle Ages is to hold the bow close to your left side while nocking. There is no advantage in it. Practice whatever system seems comfortable. Perfect it with neat gestures and a minimum of peeking.

Addressing the target: Earlier, we used the word "glare." Look at the target just as you would a mortal enemy. You might even say to yourself, "I'm going to puncture that rascal right through the gizzard!" It may sound silly, but old hands will assure you that it helps. Somehow, when you fiercely WANT to hit the mark, you are more likely to do so.

Bow-arm position: The bow is drawn against the fleshy base of the palm between the thumb and forefinger. There is no real need to twine the fingers other than lightly around the handle. The grip is best relaxed, so that the bow will turn easily for last-second adjustments in the aim.

Left: Fistmele measurement to insure proper clearance is good practice before shooting. *Right:* Nocking can become a swift, unhesitating motion using thumb and forefinger to emplace the shaft.

G. Smith

G. Smith

Three-fingered (Mediterranean) draw; relaxed hold on the bow afforded by comfortable pistol grip.

The draw: Although experimenting goes on unceasingly, most bowmen use the 3-fingered (so-called "Mediterranean") method of drawing. The forefinger is placed above the nock; the second and third fingers are placed below it. The string lies approximately across the first joint of each finger. Since pinching the nock between the fingers fouls the release, note that the pull is against the *string,* only. Fingers remain a fraction of an inch away from the nock. Do what you like with your thumb and little finger; they have no active roles, here. So relax them as best you can.

Shoulder and back muscles supply the motive power as you draw straight rearward. Your forearm is slightly high and elbow locked as you reach full draw. You will soon find the physical reason for the high arm lock; it is well nigh impossible to come to a precise stop with your forearm held low.

The hold: Here, too, is a carefully planned stage of shooting. The veteran archer may deceive you into thinking it is not. But watch him sharply. Time hangs still — even if but a fraction of a second — before he releases each shaft.

Mark well how his arrow hand comes always to the same

anchoring point on his face — and pauses. The very midpoint of the chin, a traditional hold, is preferred by most target archers. Hunters and field-course enthusiasts tend toward higher holds, such as the corner of the mouth or the cheekbone. Since these archers operate mainly without mechanical sights, it is natural they like to place the arrow nearer the eye.

Whatever your choice of hold, remember the "robot" theory: Use the same anchoring spot consistently. Or if you elect to change, do so deliberately, not by accident.

Aiming: Three distinct methods of accurate shooting are (1) point of aim; (2) instinctive ("bare bow"); and (3) free style (with mechanical sights).

Although point of aim is passing out of the picture, let's take a look at it first. It brings out two factors that must be borne in mind constantly: (1) *The eye, in shooting, is several inches above the arrow;* and (2) *the arrow, in flight, describes an arc on its way to the target.* The meaning is this: At full draw, when you look *downward* across your arrowhead, your arrow is at that very instant headed *upward.* The point of aim system demonstrates this perfectly.

Place a tennis ball, or other marker, on the ground in line between you and target. This will be your point of aim marker. Now, draw and take a line of sight across your arrowhead at the *ball,* and shoot. Observe where the arrow strikes the ground. Note that, within the bow's effective range, the point of aim marker will be somewhere between you and the striking point. (At point-blank range, the point of aim and the bull's-eye will be one and the same.)

Experiments with the point of aim will teach other lessons. Move the marker this way, or that, only a few inches. Shoot and compare. You will be thunderstruck at how widely your arrows will spray, with mere fractional deviations in aim.

"Instinctive" is a good word to describe the oldest method used by bowmen the world over. The accurate, instinctive shot is a marvelous combination of good vision; keen judgment of distance; experienced and perhaps subconscious co-ordination of

G. Smith

Bowman looks hard, almost angrily, at the mark before shooting.

G. Smith

Aiming begins as he draws downward on the target.

Draw arm high and locked to anchor point, he makes final, slight adjustments before releasing.

G. Smith

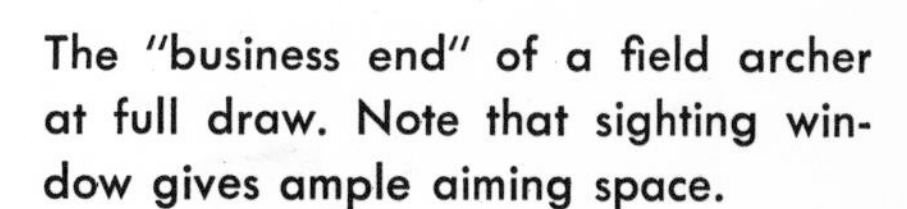

The "business end" of a field archer at full draw. Note that sighting window gives ample aiming space.

G. Smith

the mind and muscle; together with an unerring "feel" of how the particular bow and arrow will behave. Most folks who shoot the bare bow say they are aware of no fancy mental computations as they shoot. Aiming, their eyes take in the arrowhead, the bow, the target and intervening territory in one big visual image. Possibly, they say, past images flash across their mind's eye for comparison, as they adjust the final aim. When all looks "right," away she goes!

As to closing one eye or using both, the choice is yours. If you use both, you need not fear; your "master" eye will take charge, in any case; for each of us has such. Certainly there is an advantage in two-eyed aiming at longer distances. The eyes, paired, act as an excellent range finder.

Accelerating interest in target competition has inspired notable refinements in mechanical bow sights. They make it possible to reduce the guesswork in aiming. One can make micrometrically fine adjustments for yardage and horizontal traverse. There are pin-dot sights, hooded sights, crosshairs and open sights — even prisms especially designed for the long-range shots.

Bow sights bring archery a step closer to firearms shooting. The archer's eye is thus the rear sight; the mechanical aid becomes the front sight. An aiming bead is moved up or down to take care of variations in target distances. Similarly, the bead may be moved left or right, on some models, to adjust for wind influence on the arrow flight.

Another distinct feature of free-style shooting is that the bowman aims primarily through his mechanical sight. That is, he does not use his arrowhead or a point of aim.

There is no argument as to the superior accuracy of bow sights in target shooting. Scores 10 to 15 per cent better are commonly shot by free-stylers in competition with "instinct" shooters of comparable ability.

The vast majority of field and hunter bowmen continue to favor the bare bow for their phases of the sport. The prevailing sentiment is that mechanical sights are of scant advantage when a snap judgment and a lightning-fast shot has to be made, as is the case when game quarry pops out of the bushes.

G. Smith

The arrow has flown and the archer evaluates his shot. This is the follow-through of archery.

G. Smith

Typical, high-anchor point used by field shooters and hunters.

Low, mid-chin anchor point commonly used by target archers.

G. Smith

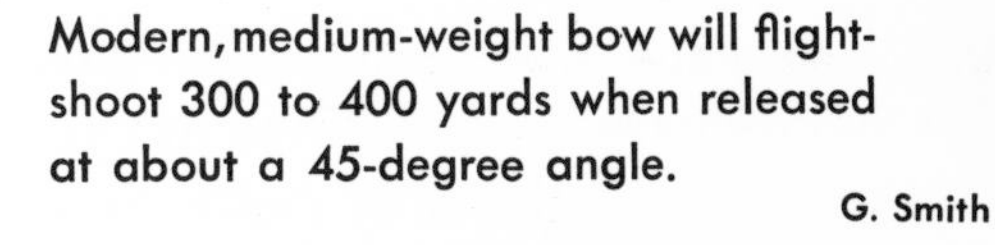

Modern, medium-weight bow will flight-shoot 300 to 400 yards when released at about a 45-degree angle.

G. Smith

G. Smith

Typical, tilted-bow style of a field archer is shown as he zeroes in on the practice butt.

The release: Here is the making or breaking place of many an archer. The release must be smooth. Crisp. Unflinching. Straightforward. Perfectly timed. By smooth, I mean no dragging, binding or rolling of the string; no pinching of the arrow nock. By crisp, I suggest a swift, one-motion relaxing of the draw fingers. By unflinching, I indicate no last-second creeping of the hand, either fore or aft. By straightforward, I plead for no sideward, upward or downward motion which could slap the arrow out of its prescribed line of flight. And lastly, let the release occur at the precise instant in time when the archer's eye signals: "Range! Mark! Shoot!"

Follow through: Other sports, such as golf, tennis and basketball, have no monopoly on this definite factor in smooth performance. Follow through adds grace to the shot, certainly. Better, it aids in subtracting any tendency to shoot frantically, desperately or nervously, whereby the archer becomes his own worst enemy. With the arrow speeding on its way, relax and enjoy it. You may go so limp as to have the bow slide out of your hand, as many experts do. At all events, use the splendid moment to follow the flying arrow throughout its course. If it's a miss, calmly reflect upon your shooting actions, seeking to find the one that did the foul deed.

Rejoice mightily if your shaft is quivering in the bull's-eye; and resolve to do it again, in exactly the same magnificent fashion!

IX

Handy Practice Setups

The gas-meter reader came up the cellar stairs with a strange look on his face.

"What'd you do? Have an Indian raid?" he asked the archer's wife.

"What makes you say that?" replied wife, expecting a joking return.

"I'll show you — if it's safe to go down there again."

In the cellar a moment later, he confronted her with Exhibit A. In a far corner hung the oblong-shaped meter. Protruding from it was the gaily colored fletching and cresting of a field arrow. Wife clapped hand over mouth, then, laughing, sized up the situation. "That husband of mine! I'm sure he didn't do it on purpose. One of his shots went wild." The gas man went away muttering.

Wife's guess was accurate. The archer confessed later he had been whiling away the winter night in his basement archery range. One shot had gotten away from him and penetrated clean through the metal casing of the meter. Ted said he had examined it to make sure the inner workings of the meter weren't damaged. Just then, an incoming, long-distance phone call put an end to the evening shoot. Friend Ted forgot all about the peculiarly lodged shaft.

In between trips afield, every archer needs facilities to keep shooting sharp. When time available is short or weather interferes, his practice must be carried on in tighter quarters, on his own home grounds, at a nearby vacant lot, or sometimes indoors. With little effort, momentary difficulties can be overcome. Workaday archers with but half an hour to spare, daily, can rig miniature ranges that afford a maximum amount of shooting.

Home basements often will accommodate 10-yard ranges with sufficient protective measures. Similarly, garages invite shooting under cover. With doors wide open and the family car removed, the garage enables a shooter to move back, outdoors, for longer ranges, the garage acting as a trap for wayward arrows. More "luxurious" indoor shooting can be achieved by organized bowmen. Working with nominal fees, club members carry on in lodge halls, gymnasiums, warehouses, bowling alleys, sports arenas and similar spacious buildings all over the country. They're set up for artificially lighted practice and competition, night or day — plus heating where the climate dictates.

Generally, target faces are sized downwards for the shorter distances. Formal competition suggests 6-, 8- and 12-inch field faces; the 16-inch size is most popular in the standard target design. For informal shooting, the sky is the limit. Witness such marks as wooden wafers, balloons, paper plates, lighted candles, swinging pendulums, and playing cards for "poker" shoots.

Aside from target faces, the main considerations of close-quarters shooting are twofold: halting arrows at the target area, and protecting the range and immediate neighborhood from arrows that go wild.

Indoors, experience indicates that floors, ceilings and side walls may need special buffering. Particular attention must be given to shields for wiring, plumbing and lighting fixtures, if they are in the danger zone. Indoors and out, close check must be made

Saunders Archery Target Co.

Simplified, "shorty" portable stand with braided 36-inch grass mat is easy to set up and an effective arrow stopper for handy practice ranges.

to eliminate protruding hard surfaces from which arrows will glance hazardously. Eliminating protrusions helps to reduce arrow breakage.

It is wise to go all out to insure a trouble-free range. Target mats and butts may be purchased. Good ones are not cheap. They are processed for maximum safety, wear and tear. Common materials are grass, straw and salt hay; also pressure-packed felt, fiber glass, and paper. Factors of arrow punishment, portability, vermin infestation, rotting, weather resistance, and price, all influence design and manufacture.

Serviceable targets can be improvised. Cramming a grocery

store carton solid-full of newspapers is one method. But examine it from time to time to make sure the stuffing hasn't shredded to the danger point. Similar results may be obtained with hard-packed sawdust, rags and wool waste.

Patrolman John Weber of Detroit, originator of the national police archery movement, writes that the home team uses bundles of corrugated cardboard, 20″ x 20″ x 12″. He says the lawmen do their own cutting and baling to save expense. The 20-by-20-inch corrugated edge surface readily absorbs and stops the policemen's arrows — even when shot from very heavy bows.

Where portability is unimportant, such as a permanent back-yard range, heavy (up to 160-pound) hay bales may be rigidly staked in place. If similar target weights are necessary on larger

Real need for portable, easy-to-carry target is met by this 10-pound fiberglass model with 25-inch face. It will stop arrows shot from 60-pound bows.

Shakespeare Co.

indoor ranges, the practice is to mount them on roller-castered platforms, for ease in moving about.

Behind the mats, butts, bales and what have you, one must reckon with arrows that miss. The idea is to stop them, undamaged. Most backstops are based on a simple principle: When an arrow strikes heavy, tough-surfaced, nonrigid material — suspended like a curtain — interesting things happen. In spite of the arrow's lethal power, it does not penetrate. Rather, the material gives, in a swing-away manner; the arrow glides downward along the billow; friction imparts a braking action; the shaft thus descends harmlessly to the ground, or floor.

Several materials for backstops have proven effective. Heavy-gauge woolen felt is most widely used. Archery houses often keep it in stock. Castoff old rugs will also do admirably. They are favored by back-yard shooters. Tarpaulins and salvaged tenting fabrics perform very well. Again, our friend, Officer Weber, says the bluecoats use discarded conveyor belting material picked up for little or nothing at steel mills and foundries.

Methods of mounting or suspending targets and backstops offer no real problems. A close look at some devices in use will reveal they can be duplicated by anyone with moderate do-it-yourself ability.

There is a commercial outgrowth of enthusiasm for handy, neighborhood ranges. At least one company is in the field of providing equipment for complete, multi-lane, indoor shooting arenas, closely resembling the familiar bowling alleys. Practice and competitions are generally based on the NAA's Chicago Round — 90 arrows (15 target ends) shot at standard, 16-inch target faces. Finishing an end, the archers press a button. The entire target butt then automatically moves on a track back to the shooting line, for safe retrieving of arrows and recording scores. Button pressing sends the target back to original position — a 14-second trip, each way.

A tackle rental and sales shop complete such setups. Archers pay as they go for shooting time. Leagues are organized and red-hot weekly contests take place. Managed by true archery enthusiasts, such enterprises do much to promote the sport.

To appease the competitive wants of indoor and short-range field-style archery, NFAA has also devised its special Twenty Yard Indoor Round. Target distances vary from twenty feet to the full twenty yards. Except for lack of outdoor locale, the Round closely follows the variable pattern of a typical field shoot. Smaller (6- and 8-inch) field faces are used. A total of 56 arrows (14 ends of 4 each) comprise a round. There's even a "walk-up" target — an end shot from four different distances.

Handy, "home-grown" range shooting offers unique opportunities. The atmosphere is often more encouraging to careful polishing of techniques than that on the bigger ranges. New equipment may be tested and mastered in leisurely fashion. The yen to tinker with tackle, targets and methods can be given complete freedom. Indeed, a miniature range can well serve as a laboratory where bright, new archery ideas first see the light of day.

Commercial archery ranges featuring push-button targets for retrieving arrows and scoring are increasing in popularity as indoor sport for the entire family.

Mobile Targets

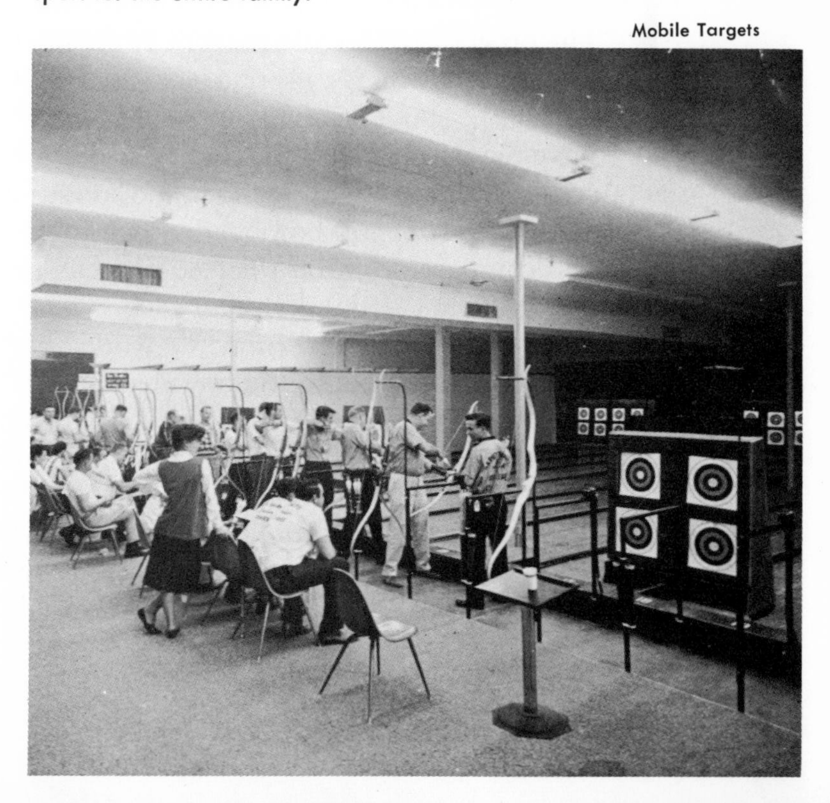

X

"Help Yourself" Department

There's an old saying that archers repeat time and time again: "The object is to hit the mark!" It means that the ultimate purpose of the bowman's myriad activities and preparations is, quite simply, to shoot straight. It would be foolish to deny this; but I have never yet met an archer who did not get equal satisfaction from "fussing" with his tackle. Eavesdrop on the conversation between a couple of bow benders, who meet about noontime. They will compare notes on their equipment until the sun sinks lower and lower in the sky.

The chance to exercise their home workshops, tools and craft skills draws many people to the bowmen's ranks. Opportunity to create and make things with the hands is wide open. If you wish, you can handcraft every item of your gear, starting from raw material, or from kits complete with how-to-do instructions.

Most archers take the middle course. They indulge in a bit of practical handiwork. Indeed they soon find a certain amount is necessary to be self-sufficient in the field. In addition, they do a great deal of hunting for accessories.

It is the selection, purchasing, adapting and fitting of new gadgets and refinements for their tackle that keep the majority of bowmen in their greatest glory, aside from shooting activity. Certainly, a real challenge exists in fabricating an item of tackle from scratch. To my mind, there is no less a challenge in continually scouting for improved aids via up-to-date archery reading, or watching the other fellow's regalia.

In any case, there's plenty of leeway to use your own knowledge and inventiveness in choosing and tailoring gadgets and materials to your particular shooting tastes.

By learning to help yourself intelligently, it is quite possible to save a dollar here and there. Mainly, though, the ideas that follow are aimed at helping you to become an independent thinker and operator at your archery hobby.

Tracing design on leather with stylus is the first step in making a pocket quiver.

G. Smith

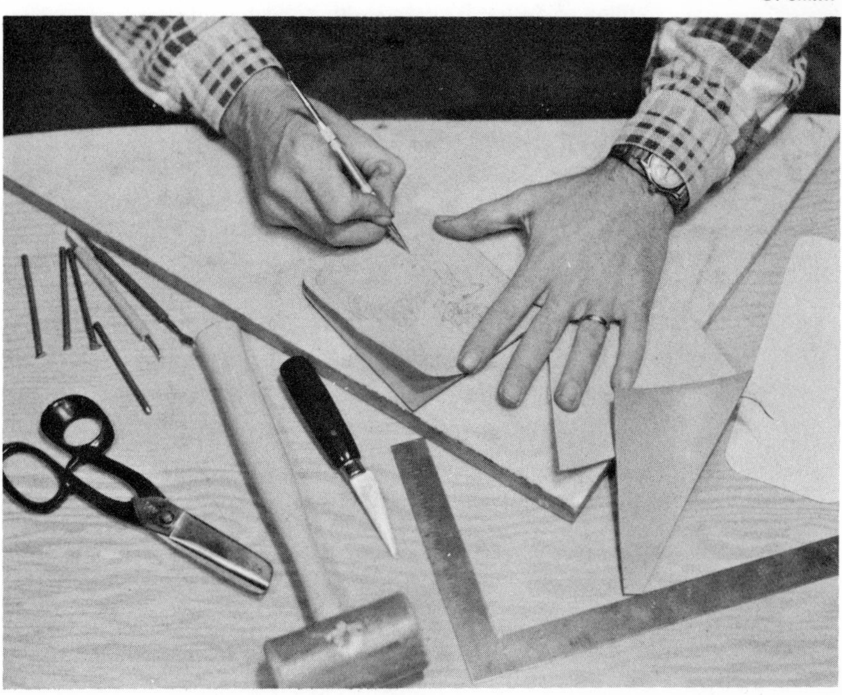

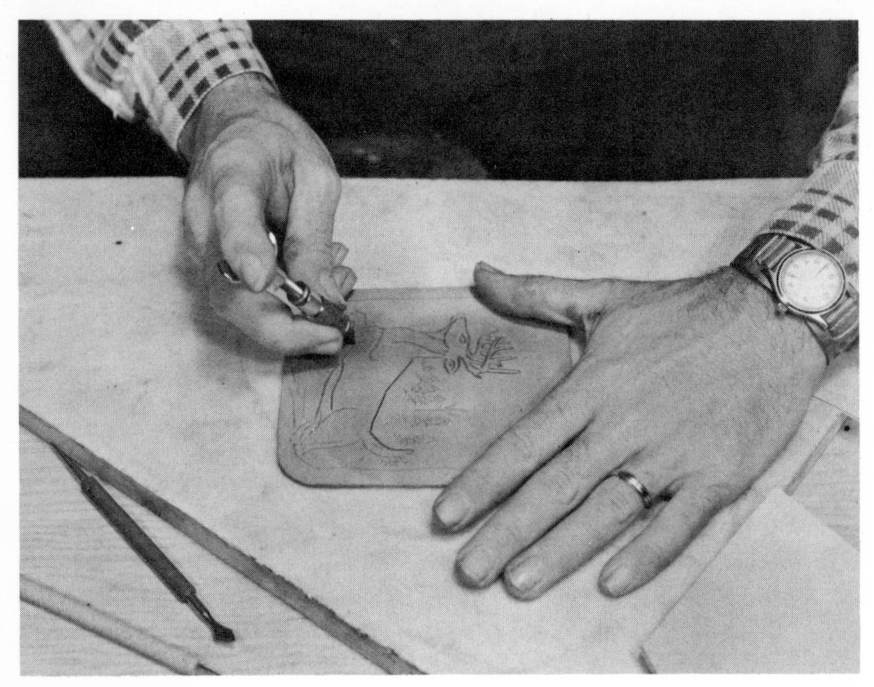

G. Smith

Outline of design is carved with a swivel knife.

A Pocket Quiver

Leather plays a big role in archery gear. Leathercraft is fun and not nearly as hard as it might appear. With experience on a simple project, the making of many leather items is possible, such as arm guards, shooting tabs, belt cases and so on. The pocket quiver is a good beginner. It's practical and affords training in all the main principles of leatherworking.

The pocket quiver is a handy accessory for the target range or field-shooting course. It will hold six arrows "at the ready" for instant stringing.

MATERIAL

Oak-tanned, medium-weight (6-7 oz.) cowhide:

1 piece 5½″ x 6″ (front of quiver)
1 piece 5½″ x 9″ (back of quiver, attaching to belt)
6 ft. of colored gimp (for lacing)

EQUIPMENT

These are basic:

1 steel try square
1 pair of heavy duty shears
1 leather-skiving knife
tracing paper
quick-drying cement

You can substitute ordinary workshop and household items for these.

1 rawhide mallet
1 orangewood stick
1 ballpoint stylus
1 stamping tool
1 thonging chisel

First, cut the front and back pieces of leather to the correct sizes. Use shears; they will snip the heaviest hide without tearing. Now, soak the pieces in water for a few hours. Then dry them. When they start regaining normal color, you can start working.

Trace the animal, bird or other design on tracing paper with pencil. Put tracing over the shorter, front piece. Have the leather smooth side up. Retrace the pencil line firmly with the ballpoint stylus. Moisten the leather surface lightly with a sponge before each tooling.

Figure carving, the next step, is the simplest form of leather tooling. Begin by using the swivel knife to go over the design outline, bringing it out strongly to the eye. Smooth out the lines; add shading and finer details with a modeling tool, or orangewood stick. When the design pleases you, you're ready to give it background.

Apply background with the stamping tool and mallet. This "puts the design in relief," as they say — gives it a third dimension. Also, stamping darkens leather and makes the figure stand

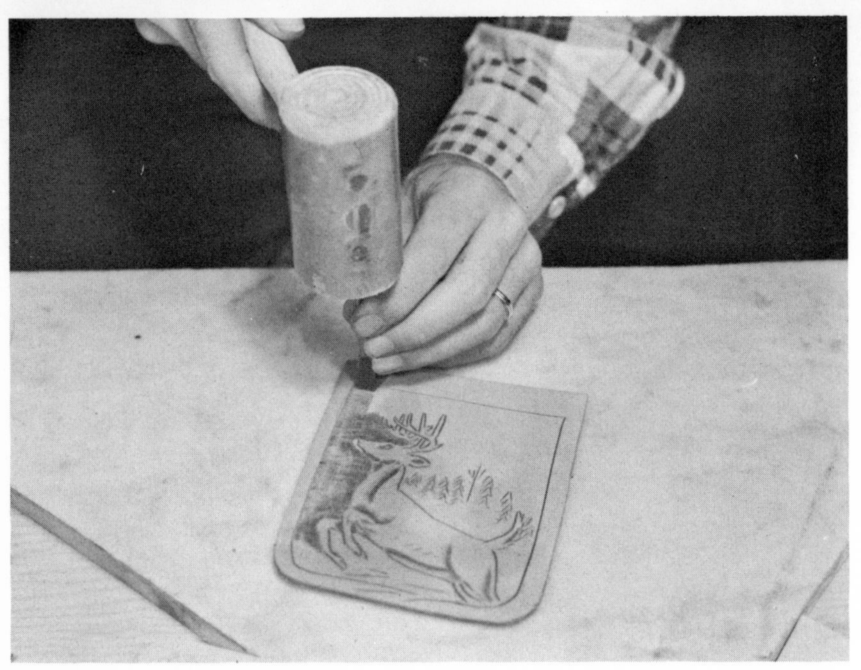

G. Smith

Background for the figure is added by hammering design in depth on wet leather.

out more sharply. The secret of stamping an even background, as shown, is to keep that mallet humming. Use quick, short strokes. Move the tool right along. Hit a bit harder wherever you want darker tones.

Complete tooling by swivel-knifing a line border around your design and background. To add "looks," do the same thing to the smooth side of the upper part of the back piece of leather. Lines should be about one-half inch from the edges.

With the knife, pare down three edges of the front piece, rough side up. This will give a neater fit to edges for lacing. Also, it bellies this piece to form a pocket.

Put holes for the lacing in both leather pieces, one-quarter inch from edges. Ordinary punches will do, but a thonging chisel is accurate and faster. Go easy on this. Try to have the holes match.

Use the knife again. Trim an area approximately 3″ x 1″ from the back piece for a more graceful appearance at the belt line.

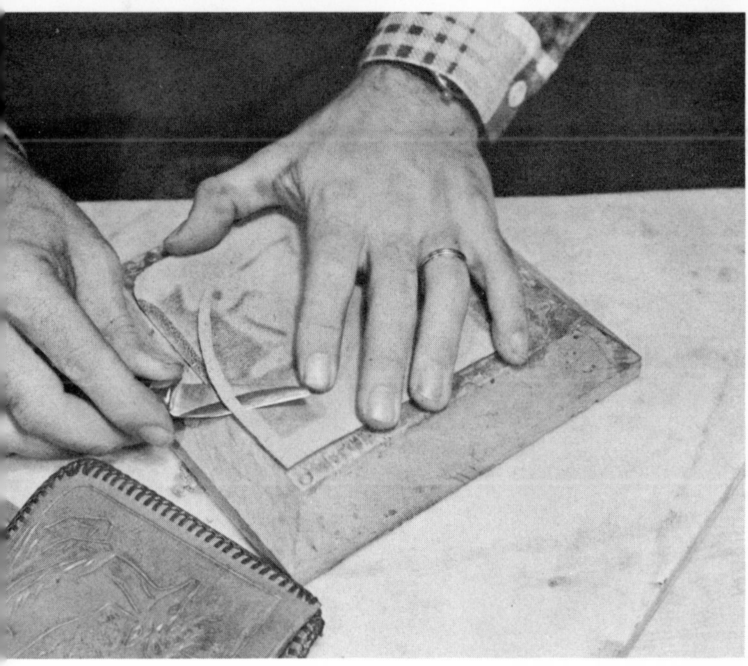

G. Smith

Edges of front piece of leather are skived for neater fitting to back.

Thonging tool makes matching holes, front and back, in preparation for lacing.

G. Smith

G. Smith

Pocket quiver holds six shafts ready for fast shooting.

Cut belt slots an inch apart in the back piece and you're all set to lace.

Of several choices in lacing methods, the continuous lay-over or buttonhole stitch seems best. It's easy to learn; it is trim and strong. Start lacing at the upper right-hand corner of the back piece. Add cement, in installments, for extra strength in lacing the joined edges of front and back pieces. When you've finished lacing, flatten and smooth it by pounding gently all the way around.

For best results, work on a steady table. Do stamping and tooling on a smooth piece of marble, slate, or heavy plate glass. Do cutting and punching on a block of wood. Prime tools are the knife, shears and try square. You can easily adapt ordinary nails, nail punches, screw drivers and awls for leatherworking.

Don't make the mistake of buying *minerally* tanned (chrome) leather for this or any tooling project. It has to be *vegetably* tanned.

Arrows, the Easy Way

Archery is an economical sport. Once an initial investment is made in good equipment, the outlay from there on is modest. However, there is one unavoidable hole in the budget. Arrows have a habit of breaking, lodging in the tops of unclimbable trees, hiding in brush and grass, and just drifting off into the never-never land.

Arrowsmith begins task by giving shafts a light coat of clear lacquer.

G. Smith

At present shop prices, fair-grade "expendables" cost around 75¢ apiece. Custom-made, deluxe target and hunting arrows in matched sets are priced up to $3 each. It is no trick at all to "burn up" a half-dozen or so missiles in a day's shooting. Especially, before one gets good at placing shots.

For these and other reasons, we suggest you learn to do a bit of arrowsmithing. Methods described here are simple and fast; equipment needed is not costly.

Listing the ingredients below, we deliberately do not mention shaft diameters, shaft lengths, type of head and spine measurements. You, as an individual, will have to make your own decision on these matters, from information elsewhere in the book. Now, collect the following:

MATERIALS

1 half-pint can of clear lacquer
1 dozen shafts of Port Orford cedar
1 dozen plastic nocks
1 dozen arrowheads of your own selection
3 dozen feather or plastic vanes
1 tube, quick-drying cement
1 stick, ferrule cement

TOOLS

1 sheet of very fine sandpaper
1 hobby knife, single-edge razor blade or other ultra-sharp instrument
1 narrow brush for lacquer
1 fletching jig (or several, to speed the job)
1 feather-burning jig (or skip, if plastic vanes used)
1 tapering tool (if nocks or heads require it)
1 pair pliers
1 ordinary tavern candle

With this assembled, you can easily mass-produce a dozen serviceable, 3-vane arrows in a couple of hours.

As you work, follow the sequence of steps as indicated. For instance do *not* cut off shaft excess immediately. You'll need it for a *dry* handhold when lacquering, and otherwise finishing up.

G. Smith

Tenon tool works like pencil sharpener in shaping shaft ends for arrow points and nocks.

G. Smith

Nock is emplaced at right angles to the grain, using a dab of cement.

Sharp scissors and steel rule are used to cut feathers to proper vane length — 5 inches in the case of these field arrows.

G. Smith

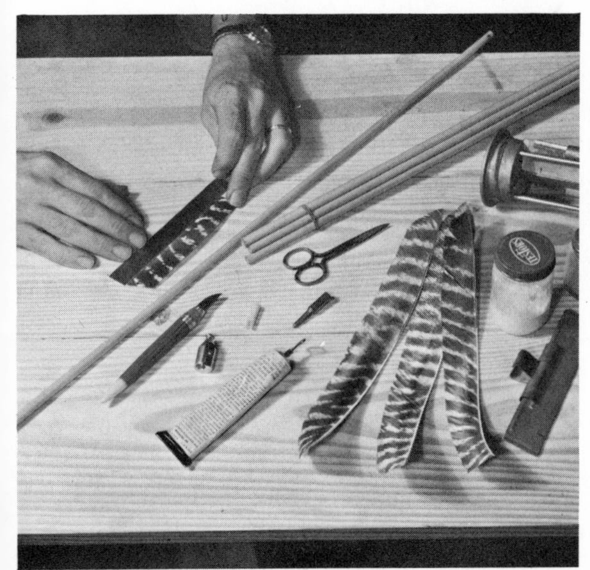

Cement is applied to base of the feathers. They are then clamped to the shaft emplaced in the jig.

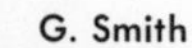
G. Smith

G. Smith

Feather burner in action is spectacular, and gives off a hearty "wet-dog" type of odor.

First, let's get the nocks on. To place them properly, look closely for the grain of the shaft wood. Find it by examining one end. You'll want the grain to run at right angles to the bow. The reason is, this will take best advantage of the spine (stiffness) in your shafts. Mark the grain location with your thumbnail or lightly with pencil. Bear in mind this is where your cock feather will eventually be attached.

Back to the nocks. Taper the end of the shaft, if your nock requires that type of fitting. Put a blob of the quick-drying cement on the shaft end. Install the nock with a twisting motion, positioning it according to your previous mark for the grain. Apply all nocks in this fashion. Number one will be quite dry when you come back to it for the next operation.

Apply one smooth, generous coat of lacquer to the shaft. Allow time for drying and then lightly sand off the flaky, rough spots.

Place a shaft in the fletching jig. The position of the nock must be co-ordinated with the positions of the one cock- and two hen-vanes. Remember, the cock-vane will be attached where you marked the grain, earlier; the hen-vanes to either side of it. You can decide here and now whether you want your cock-vane to be brighter or different in color from the hens. Color may aid you in getting an arrow strung right side up for rapid shooting situations.

Quick-drying cement will hold the vanes on. Spread it on the base of the vanes, first. Stick vanes to shaft. Clamp for drying.

If you have chosen ready-shaped, plastic vanes, you may skip the next step. Or, again, you may have shaped your vanes with scissors; or bought ready-cut feathers.

G. Smith

Roll-as-you-cut is the approved method of achieving squared-off, unsplintered shafts.

G. Smith

Alcohol torch or tavern candle serve equally well for heat needed to affix heads with ferrule cement.

Otherwise, plug in the electric, feather-burning jig. By now you have probably discovered that the burner element can be bent to give you any shape of vane you desire.

Put the rough-feathered shaft in the metal couch and revolve it to make sure it will trim the feather at the right area without charring your shaft. Then, turn on the "juice" and enjoy the "wet dog" smell of carbonized feathers. Note the burner works fast. Keep the shaft revolving to avoid a flame-up!

Since it's good practice to order shafts one size (2 inches) too long, this is the moment to get rid of the extra length. Measure carefully to fit your requirement and note the following technique to achieve a clean, square cut: Use your hobby knife or other sharp edge. Lay shaft on a sturdy, smooth surface. Protecting the vanes, roll the shaft beneath the edge of your blade. Cut as you roll, deepening the cut gradually.

After a couple of revolutions, you will find the cedar shaft easy to snap between your fingers. There may be a few center fibers left for you to trim off cleanly. On the other hand, attempting to slice through solely from one direction results in uneven cuts and splintering.

The interior bore of your arrowhead will determine your next move. If the bore is cone-shaped, you will need to taper the head of the shaft, using the special tool much as you would a pencil sharpener. Should your head have a parallel (or call it cylindrical) bore, you may need to sand the shaft for fitting. Do so very lightly in order not to weaken it.

Light the candle and melt a blob of ferrule cement onto the shaft head. With pliers to protect your hands, heat the arrowhead for a couple of minutes. Working quickly, slide the head onto the shaft while the cement is still molten. Seizing the shaft as close to the point as possible — to keep it from breaking — jam the head against a solid obstacle such as the workbench. As it cools, the head will shrink, affording a sound, tight force fitting. Excess cement around the joint may be reheated and scraped off.

Cresting and other marking (discussed elsewhere in these pages) may now be added, if desired.

The above methods will produce inexpensive arrows for any purpose, whether it be target practice, roving, field-archery competition or hunting.

Fish-shooting Rigs

Although not all states have yet legalized bow and arrow pursuit of carp, gar, eels, herring, bullheads, frogs and the like, gains are made each passing year. The pursuit adds zest to archery pleasures and sharpens shooting skills. For the handyman, it provides still another chance to fashion his own gear. Make sure that you are within the law before you go out to use your gear.

You can buy a complete bow-fishing outfit, consisting of reel, line, and fish arrow for a moderate sum. However, there are numerous combinations of gear you can rig up yourself, try, and adjust. Your experiments may pay off in just the outfit that suits your favorite type of water archery.

Reels: All are based on the spinning-reel principle familiar to conventional fishermen. In action, the line pays off sideways with a minimum of friction or danger of snagging. Models seen on the market can easily be duplicated by the home craftsman. I made one out of a plastic drinking cup. Another fellow in the gang shaped an arbor from a block of wood. Still another cut one from a section of aluminum stovepipe. Each of us simply added a pair of "feet" (or bracket) to his reel, as a means of attaching same to our bows. The stovepipe model is a "shoot-through" job. The others mentioned are taped to positions above or below the arrow rest.

To my reel, I added a little spring clip. It keeps the line from falling off the reel while I'm looking for an unwary carp or other target. It releases under pressure of the arrow leaving the bow.

Line: This is heavier than would be used for ordinary fishing. The reason is, if you miss your prey the arrow reaches the end of the line with great force. Therefore, use 75-pound test, kinkproof, nylon line. It comes in 75-foot spools, which is plenty long enough; most shots are made at less than half that range.

If you are working on toothy fish, such as alligator gar, you would be wise to add three feet of 100-pound test, braided wire leader to the forward end of your line.

In any case, connection of the line to the arrow leader by means of a steel or brass snap-swivel is helpful. This enables you to detach your arrow quickly for removal of an impaled fish; or to make your rig handier to carry from one place to another.

Arrow shafts: It is possible to use regular shaft material such as wood or tubular glass and aluminum. Better results are obtained with solid shafts of glass or aluminum, as they are not buoyant in water. Length of shaft should be ample to clear the head from the back of the bow, or to prevent barbing your bow hand when you come to full draw. As to fletching, many water shooters feel it is not essential and that it slows down the arrow when submerged. You are welcome to test your own theory. However, special rubber fletching is available; it slides over the shaft. Feather fletching may be waterproofed with one of the several brands of spray material.

Fishing heads: There are a bewildering array of special points for the fishing archer. They fall readily into three general types. One type is the solidly attached, fixed barb head; you must "worry" or cut it out of the fish, or pass it all the way through, shaft, fletching and all. Another type has fixed barbs, but is readily detachable; you shove it through the fish, unscrew the head, then withdraw the shaft from the other direction. The third type has movable, removable, or reversible barbs. A simple motion gets barbs out of the way. I like a reversible stingaree. It is easily withdrawn, even when the head is completely buried in a fish's carcass.

In a pinch, you can make a reserve supply of fishing heads from ordinary field points. File or grind each to a sharp nose. Drill a hole behind the nose to receive a 2-inch length of heavy piano wire, snipped to create sharp ends. Insert wire and bend backward in barb fashion. Peen the wire into solid position, using a machinist's hammer.

Fishing heads are otherwise seated on shafts in the same manner as other types of arrows.

Attachment methods: I have found that ordinary draftsman's masking tape is the best means of holding the reel to my weapon. It is amply strong, and does not leave a messy residue, as some tapes do. To insure that neither the fish nor the reel get away from you, tie the rear end of the line to the *bow.*

Leader line may be hitched to the arrow in one of three ways. One is through a hole near the head. Another is through a hole near the nock. The third method, which I favor, involves use of a hole near the head *and* a hole near the nock: Tie line through the forward hole, then pass rearward and tie it through a hole to

E. DeRienze

Rubber bow boot saves wear at the tip. Brush button keeps string from snagging in brush.

E. DeRienze

Periodic applications of ordinary furniture wax maintain bow finish; give weapons longer life.

the rear of the shaft. This creates a sort of "harness" which I feel results in a more stabilized flight of the arrow.

Fishing bows: No special weapon or adaptation is required. Select one with ample power to overcome resistance encountered by the arrow under water. I'd recommend using your "second" bow if you have such. Tramping amid swamps and river banks or banging around in a boat is likely to be rough on your most prized armament.

Care of Your Bow

Your weapon will last for many years with reasonable protection from weather and damage. Light applications of furniture wax will preserve its finish. Wipe on with a soft cloth. When carrying it from place to place, cut down on wear and tear by using a bow case. Avoid laying the bow on the ground; it will pick up moisture and may get stepped on. Acquire "bow boots" or similar protectors for the tips.

At the end of a day's shooting give your bow a good home. Install wall pegs or a rack where your equipment may repose safe from injury until the next outing.

About Bowstrings

For the make-it-yourself-all-the-way enthusiast, suppliers will furnish spools of bowstring material together with step-by-step directions. Prestretched dacron is most common. The number of strands used per string depends upon the test strength indicated by the manufacturer. Test strength of the finished string is usually 5 times the draw weight of the bow. Thus, a 50-pound bow will take a 250-pound test string. Order a ready-made string by giving the weight of your bow and the bow length. Get the latter figure

Cotton thread wound around primary serving at center of bowstring gives bowman a precise point to nock his arrow.

E. DeRienze

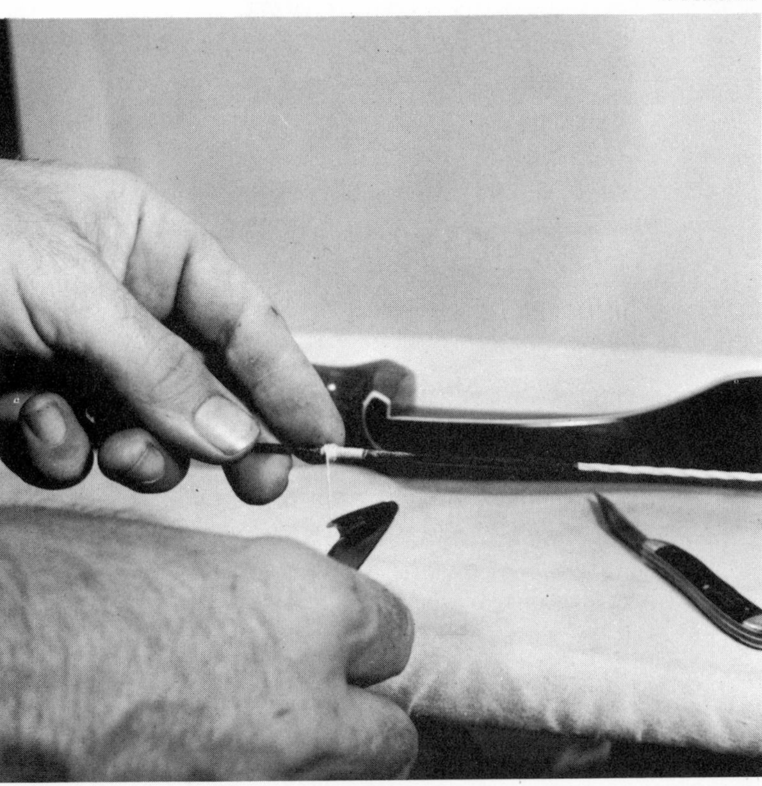

G. Smith

Carefully beeswaxing the string before each shooting session is a good ritual to follow. Fraying and breakage are prevented.

accurately by measuring with a tape, nock to nock, along the *back* of the bow.

Arrow-nocking points are a must. They give an exact location from which arrows are launched from the string. They are applied over the serving (primary wrapping) near the center of the string. Use a carpenter square to find a right angle that runs from your string across the arrow rest. Tie one end of a length of cotton thread 1/8-inch above this spot. Apply a dab of model cement. While it is still wet, wind the thread around and around until a hump is built up. Now, continue winding upward, the width of an arrow nock; here, wind up another hump, adding more cement. Now tie off the thread, and the job is done. When nocked properly, the arrow will cling snugly until it is shot.

It is very important that the string, in braced position, be stationed a proper distance from the bow. This measurement is usually prescribed by the bow manufacturer. If not, try the fistmele method: Put the base of your fist to the belly (or "inside") of the bow, extending the thumb toward the string. The latter should clear the thumb comfortably. For a more ample fistmele, give the string a twist or two; this will tighten it.

Store-bought rubber nocking points can be put on with little difficulty, with the aid of a hairpin. The hairpin is slipped through a loop of the bowstring, and is used as a needle in threading a pair of rubber sleeves over the string. Sleeves are slid to the nocking position. A gap left between them creates the exact nocking point.

Rubber "gadgets" also serve to silence strings for hunting purposes. They are emplaced in pairs, one for an area in each half of the bowstring where maximum vibration takes place. Reduced vibration cuts down noise.

Arrow Finishing and Maintenance

Precision fletching jigs and gauges run into money but pay off in truer-flying shafts. They insure exact placement of whatever number of vanes are required, for any degree of right- or left-hand spiral. Clamps are held on magnetically and permit superior bonding between fletching and shaft. Vanes are glued on with great care, one at a time.

Fletching and cresting for all types of shaft material had best be preceded with a thin coat of clear lacquer. For complete success, aluminum needs particular attention. Handle the tubing with cotton gloves. This keeps natural oils in the hands from smearing the surface. First, lightly buff the shaft with abrasive paper. Dip it in the lacquer. When dry, rub lightly with steel wool. Then proceed as with other materials, still keeping bare hands off.

Colorful, automotive lacquers or model enamels do well for cresting. Shafts may be dipped or brushed. Ring-around designs — neat and precise — call for a remarkably steady hand at the striping brush. This problem can be solved with homemade gadgetry or store-bought, electric-powered equipment. Home craftsmen build workable units from castoff clock spring mechanisms. A nock receiver is affixed to the driveshaft, turning over at about 250 revolutions per minute. The far end of the arrow shaft is supported by a wire cradle. A rest is provided for the brush hand. In this fashion, any number of rings of varying width and color are applied swiftly.

For a really fast cresting job, get decals. When wetted in the usual manner, they readily slide onto shafts. Dried slowly and thoroughly, then sprayed with clear plastic, they give good service. Luminous colors make for excellent visibility.

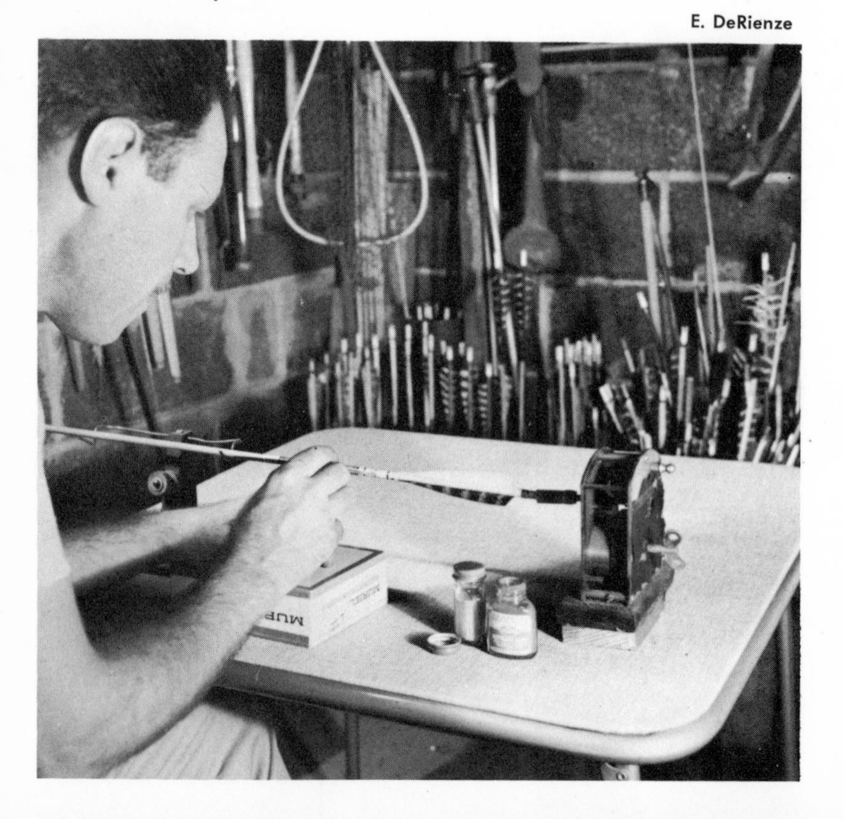

Professional-grade cresting is achieved by this archer-craftsman using a spring mechanism devised to spin shafts at about 250 revolutions per minute.

E. DeRienze

Comfort, convenience and the type of shooting you anticipate should govern your choice of quiver. Targeteers lean toward smaller, belt or other waistline models. Field and hunter archers tend to pack their more numerous arrows higher on the body and thus in roomier designs.

The target specialist's quiver needs hold no more than an "end" of six arrows. However, it must suit him as to easiness of reach and bodily freedom for unobstructed shooting.

Afield, the bowman reckons he is likely to lose or break arrows; a reasonable supply must be accommodated. Broadheads may require reinforcement. Rattling of shafts may need silencing, if game is in the offing. For travel through brush, thought must be given to designs that minimize snagging. Ease of rapid shooting raises yet another standard.

"Try on" before buying is the wisest course. Go through motions of drawing an arrow, shooting, stooping, walking, sliding through bushes, and whatever other typical situations you envisage. Think of the cold days when the quiver needs adjustment over heavier clothing. Think of the hot days, too, when that oversize shoulder quiver may scorch the hide off your back. Insist that your wants be met. You may not buy another quiver for many a day.

XI

Competition Shooting

"Who is the best shot in the crowd?" The question may be partly answered in many different kinds of contests. "Partly" because it's rare that one person excels at all the myriad forms of shooting.

Saxton Pope's Indian companion, Ishi, scored poorly on standard target faces. But, let a wild pig wander in front of his bow; then, Ishi's aim was devastating. Myself, I've always had trouble at ultrashort ranges, such as the small game silhouettes at a field shoot. Yet, my morale goes up at the 60-yard shots. By some twist of ability, I find I can lob them in there, often a little better than the other guy. Persist in matching your skills with fellow bowmen, and I suspect you'll find your "meat" somewhere along the line.

The two major forms of competitive activity are Target Archery and Field Archery. In the first, *targets* of uniform size are shot on an open, level field, with the line of shooters moving in unison from one fixed and known distance to another. *Field targets,* on the other hand, are only *somewhat* uniform in size, and are shot at over rough and often wooded terrain. Small squads of bowmen follow each other from one target to another, much as golfers move around the country club links. Again, field target distances vary widely within each course and are known to competing bowmen in only a general way.

Target Contests

Much historical spirit has been retained in modern target tournaments. Somehow, it remains in the atmosphere, although glittering kings, princes and princesses — who used to sponsor such events — have long since gone, together with their shining knights in armor and grim-faced men-at-arms. Yet, rich tradition lingers in the formalities, rules, conduct of the officials, and the crisply organized shooting.

Colorful too is the picture presented by a target field when competition is afoot. Bright-hued flags flutter in the wind above the line of target butts at one side of the field. Across the green turf opposite, the shooters are arrayed — predominantly clothed in white sport togs, their equipment sparkling in the sun. A long parade rank of archers methodically, gracefully addresses arrows to the target. Back of them, an equal number await their turn. Still further back are the spectators, watching through field glasses or moving feverishly about for a better view of each target lane.

Like long streaks of silver rain, the arrows slash, hiss and sputter upon the paper and straw of the marks. Great, woolly white clouds drift slowly across the blue sky. Below, the shooting pressure and excitement mounts, punctuated by the Field Captain's whistle blasts. Then there are intervals for marching to the targets and jotting down scores. Altogether, there's a panorama worthy of any artist's brush.

There are a dozen or more different target rounds and related events. In addition, there are special adaptations for men, women, intermediates, juniors, cadets and beginners, as well as for both

The Author

Women shoot a Double American Round at regional tournament held at Lancaster, Pennsylvania.

indoor and outdoor shooting. Certain rounds are devised for international tourneys and "mail shoots." (In the latter case, two archery clubs separated by distance agree to shoot on a certain day; then send each other scores for comparison and adjudging winners.)

In the U. S. A., the American Round is popular and used as an index of archery skill. It consists of 30 arrows shot at each of three distances — 60, 50 and 40 yards. To be top-classed as "AA" shooters, men must post an official score of at least 700 in the American; at least 1400 in the Double American. Women rated AA must score at least 1300 in the Double.

Young archers do not ordinarily compete with adults in official NAA contests until they reach 18. At ages 15 through 17, an archer fires the American Round as an Intermediate; at 12 through 14 as a Junior, and at 11 as a Cadet or Beginner. Juniors and Cadets shoot special Target Rounds, such as the Junior American. Distances are ten yards shorter than the standard American Round.

A recent Junior Champion, Jim Leder of Cincinnati, shoots a 1469, full-scale Double American. His score is among the nation's best target scores — adult or junior.

Customarily, four archers are assigned to each target. They step to the shooting line in pairs. One pair shoots three arrows apiece; then steps back to allow the other pair to shoot likewise. They repeat the cycle; thereupon each has shot six arrows (equaling one "end"). On signal from the Field Captain, they stride to the standard 48-inch, circular target. One bowman acts as target captain; another shooter (sometimes two of them) records the scores.

The target captain withdraws arrows for each shooter, one at a time, calling the score, beginning with the highest value. (Cresting on arrows identifies owners.)

The Gold bull's-eye at the center scores 9. From the bull outward, the circles are scored: Red — 7, Blue — 5, Black — 3, White — 1. The value of each individual hit is recorded on the score cards, so that the arithmetic can be double-checked for accuracy. Results of a target contest are thus expressed in two figures: one for the number of hits and one for the totaled scoring values.

An interesting phase of target archery is the Clout Shoot. The target is flat on the ground. The trick is to lob arrows in from *above,* a carry-over from medieval warfare. Scoring is the same as for other normal rounds. This is long-range shooting — 180 yards and 36 arrows (6 ends). Only the center of the huge 48-foot target face is marked; hit values are reckoned by measuring distances off center.

Flight shooting, too, has its fascination. It requires more elbow room than is commonly available. The objective is purely distance. That means at least 300 yards for a run-of-the-mill target bow and nearly 800 yards for the specialized, ultrapowerful flight bow shot by means of bracing it against the feet while lying on your back!

As befits an older form of the sport, target archery has more formality, a sharper refinement of discipline. By no means is it unduly severe. There is plenty of shop talk and social talk between competitors, with much top-notch sportsmanship displayed. Yet, in contrast to field archery, there is a notably higher rate of interest in the finer details of shooting and in the technical aspects of equipment.

A target contest is very much an archer's research laboratory. A stroll among the tackle boxes and along the shooting line is likely to reward one with an up-to-the-second exposure to the very latest developments, together with a view of things to come.

Finally, let no one discount the physical strain placed upon targeteers. The field may appear serene, particularly with half the shooters momentarily ensconsed in lawn chairs. But let any man test his muscular endurance on such as the Double York Round in the course of a day. That's 288 arrows, including 144 shot at the 100-yard range. The necessary hiking is five or six miles.

Field Shoots

The rise of field archery has lifted bow sport into the ranks of big time recreational industry. The lively market created by thousands of new recruits in field shooting has enabled tackle makers to double and redouble production. It has encouraged them to research frantically for improved materials and designs. There is no doubt that today's wide availability of superlative bows and arrows at reasonable cost is due to the mass purchasing power of archers drawn to this newer phase of the sport.

Field shooting is based on the bowman's unquenchable urge to rove, to hunt, to "plink" (as riflemen put it), to exert his prowess as a marksman on whatever chance target presents itself. You will see this spirit embodied in the emblem of the NFAA, the

Olde Stump riddled with arrows. There is historical evidence that archers through the centuries played the roving game. Casting one's thoughts back to Merrie England, one can imagine hearing a Locksley man say, "See the squirrel on the bole of yonder oak? I'll pin him with one clothyard bodkin and dare ye to do like-wise!" In nothing flat a medieval field-archery bout would be under way.

At more than 2,000 field courses now set up in the U. S. A. and Canada, you will see evidence of the great desire to learn hunting techniques. Targets and target lanes are laid out in a manner that will approximate actual wild game habitat. There is a studied attempt to give shooters good exercise in puffing up and down hills, crossing streams, and identifying "game" in unexpected places.

Target lanes extend through brush, high grass, tangled thickets, desert and open country. Stakes indicating shooting positions are fiendishly emplaced; they force archers to stoop, squat, kneel and bend, backwards and forwards. Further to deny him any easy, shooting-gallery technique, the bowman is required to switch from one side of the stakes to the other, in successive go-arounds.

Your first shooting journey around a field course is bound to be hectic. However, you will soon note there is order amid all the seeming confusion. For instance, 14 target lanes make a shooting unit; 28 target lanes make up a complete shooting round. The number of shooting units on any course will depend on the area available, or again, on the respective club's interest in maintaining more than the minimum. It takes work to keep a field range in shape.

Distances range between 20 feet and 80 yards. NFAA prescribes the numbers of targets, face sizes and pertinent distances — but the arrangement of these is left to each club's discretion. This is because local terrain must be taken into account. The result is a fascinating variation from one club course to another.

Field shooters proceed from one target lane to another in squads numbering no more than five bowmen. Each, in rotation, shoots four arrows at one target, or — as the case may be — at

The Author

Deer silhouette cut from laminated composition board hung from trolleys on a guy wire . . .

four separate targets. By common consent, one archer pulls arrows from the target face, calling the hits and values; another squad member records the tally on individual score cards.

Field scoring is related to hunting. Either you kill the game, or wound or miss it. Therefore, in the Field and Hunter Rounds, a killing shot counts 5; a wounding shot counts 3. Faces in these rounds are circular and vary in size from 6 to 24 inches. The outer ring for the Field Round is black; the bull is white with a black center spot. The Hunter Round target has an all-black background with a white aiming spot in the center.

The nature of targets and scoring are different for the Animal Round. Faces are hand-drawn or colorfully lithographed representations of familiar wild game animals and birds, ranging from moose to prairie dogs. Long shots include the bigger creatures.

The Author

. . . plus a bicycle wheel, sprocket, chain and pedal drive with which to propel the unit back and forth . . .

Smaller species make up the close shots. Oblong-shaped "killing areas" are marked out on each, measuring anywhere from 2 1/4 to 9 inches wide; the remainder of the critter, to the hide or feather line, counting as a "wound area."

At each target position, Animal Round shooters are allowed only three arrows. The individual must cease shooting as soon as he has hit either of the scoring areas. A hit with the first arrow counts 20 in the kill area — 16 as a wound. Second arrow counts 14 or 10. The third tallies 8 or 4.

Clubs take great pride in adding new challenge to their courses and contests. Rounds are enhanced by mechanical gadgetry that gives bowmen practice on simulated running deer, bounding rabbits and flying ducks. Other field-shooting spice is added by having contestants attired as Indian braves, Robin Hood's men, and

The Author

. . . furnishes would-be hunters a splendid chance to sharpen their skill at bringing down game at the gallop.

what have you. As big-game season approaches, many clubs set up facilities for broadhead shooting. This requires special butts and backstops for safety and to protect the keen edges of these murderous missiles.

As with target archery, field shooters are classified according to ability for fairness in competition. The bowman's best official score in either the Field or Hunter Round is used as an index. The top rating is "EXAA." To achieve this, men must score 400 upwards. For women, it is 275 upwards.

In field archery, young archers begin to compete with adults at age 16, though there are many organizations that feel there should be a special category for archers under 18. Field archers between 13 and 15 are Intermediates. Under 12, the field archer is a Junior. Field Rounds are scaled down only for the juniors; shooting stakes are placed nearer to the targets.

Field Round scores for current Intermediate Boy champions run consistently over 500 in the free-style (sight) division.

The Fraternity of Archers

Underneath all the outward differences, there is a strong bond of interest and experience between target and field archers. With few exceptions, for example, the jargon used either on the target range or the field course is the same. True it is that a targeteer's "end" is six arrows, while a field shooter's is four; but this merely illustrates how trivial the language problems are. Otherwise, words like "creep," "cast," "anchor," "fistmele," and so on, are universally understood, whatever the archer's prime interest.

Barring a few specialty items, such as the ground quiver for targets and the back quiver for the field, shooting equipment differs little. At one time, field men shot considerably heavier

Detroit police archers are among the nation's best. Teams coached by Patrolman John Weber *(not shown)* have taken top awards. *Left to right:* Detective Jess Shick; Sergeant W. Owen; Sergeant Pat Burgin; and Inspector DeLuca.

Detroit Police Dept.

bows. With the advent of supercast, light-draw models, the contrast is fading out of the picture. Flat trajectories of the newer weapons afford wide versatility.

Although bow sights appear more frequently in target tournaments, they are not unusual on the field course. Free-style (sights) and instinctive (bare bow) events are scheduled in both branches of competition.

There is considerable similarity too in the amount of shooting that target and field archers customarily pack into a day of competition. Four to five hours of bow bending, in one session, appears to satisfy targeteers and field enthusiasts alike. The interval allows for coverage of a 28-target field round; or a double shooting of a target round such as the American. This includes latitude for practice, a refreshment break, judging and awarding of prizes.

Boundary lines between target and field interests are being crossed more often as time goes along. Many clubs are encouraging both kinds of competition among their members.

Now that archers of all specialties are getting together in spite of their different preferences, they are bringing about many improvements in public and official views of archery. Bow hunting and fishing laws are being liberalized, and you hear more talk of including archery preserves in natural resource planning.

XII

Be an Archer-Explorer

The world of archery invites endless exploration. A few archers will actually go on exotic trips for bow sport, such as jaguar hunting in South America. Still others will get to know the beautiful target greens of Europe through travel and competition with bowmen of other nations.

But the majority, by far, will be those archers who explore mainly nearer home. Much of our "exploring" will be in search of further information. Archery has become so dynamic, fast growing and ever changing in trends, it is imperative to keep a constant vigil. Alertness is rewarded by more shooting enjoyment and a sense of growing along with the sport.

Organization Aids

To move more quickly into midstream of archer news, by all means join a local club. Archery clubs are usually affiliated with national, regional, or state associations. Through these channels flows a steady current of intelligence regarding competitions, hunting and fishing seasons, new equipment, and forecasts of things to come.

For an example of its informative value — our own state archery association mails monthly bulletins on the location and nature of upcoming shoots, meetings; legislation affecting the bow; notes on tackle improvements. In addition, the association publishes an annual directory of club courses and ranges, including competition rules and a complete calendar of scheduled activities.

For an over-all outlook on archery in the U. S. A., consider joining a national organization. Following are current addresses:

National Archery Association of the United States: This is the first-organized federation of American archery groups and is devoted to target competition. By arrangement with the publisher, significant NAA news is released through *The Archers' Magazine* (TAM). Membership automatically provides a subscription to this periodical. For further details regarding NAA membership and subscriptions to TAM, communications may be sent to P. O. Box 832, Norristown, Pa.

National Field Archery Association: This is the group for the field archer and bowman hunter. Its monthly magazine, *Archery,* covers the game trails and field shoots all over America. Write to Post Office Box H, Palm Springs, Calif.

American Bowhunters Association, Inc.: This membership is beamed directly at hunting with the bow and all means of improving the sport, including the testing, evaluation and promotion of suitable tackle. Write to Sportsman's Haven, Route 1, Alpena, Mich.

Bowhunting: Here is a monthly magazine that covers interests of the several national associations and numerous regional archery groups, including target, field and the hunt. Write to 29 Allegheny Avenue, Towson 4, Md.

For a Broader Viewpoint

Deeper, more satisfying exploration of the archer's world and its history, as related arts and sciences, may await you at your library. Historians have dug up surprisingly detailed accounts of the bow in action, down through the centuries, in all corners of the globe. Encyclopedias will help satisfy your curiosity. Books on travel to remote places may reveal other bits of information.

Museums of one type and another often afford much of interest to the archer. Paintings, sculpture and other art work of the past frequently use the archer theme. The most famous example of this is the 76-yard-long tapestry at Bayeux, France; it reveals much unique information about the archers' battle between Normans and Saxons fought at Hastings in England, in the year 1066.

Collections of weapons displayed at historical museums sometimes include bows and arrows. Such exhibits may even provide ideas that can be adapted to modern tackle. There is plenty of evidence that commercial tackle manufacturers are awake to this possibility. Recurves, composites, sighting windows, bow quivers, special arrow points — you are likely to see these and many another "modern" archery development reflected in a casual tour through relics of the past.

XIII

Bow Sport Conservation

As a professional conservationist ranging regularly over a goodly part of the U. S. A., I run across mounting evidence that archers are a real asset to programs of resource protection. I am referring to the nation's interest in guarding, improving and using wisely our soil, water, forests and wildlife, including our fisheries.

Anyone can see and sense what is happening to our priceless heritage in this era of frantic development of homes, schools, industries, shopping centers, highways, airports, missile bases and you name it. With population growth bursting at the seams, something has had to give. The "giving" has been taking place at breathless speed in the once-unspoiled woodland, open, farm countryside, and along the formerly sparkling stream.

Each year, our agriculture alone loses some three million acres of prime soils to the pavers and roofers.

As the "squeeze" closes in about us, it seems to me that bow sport takes on greater significance. Bow hunters operate safely and efficiently in those smaller parcels of land often stranded in the onrush of urbanization. At his deadliest within 25 to 35 yards of his quarry, the bowman needs but an acre or two for a small game hunt. He can bag bunnies in a neighborhood woodlot, knock off rats in the town dump, and scarcely attract attention. His silent, stalking method contrasts sharply with the firing and bustle of a conventional gun hunt.

Big game fields comfortably absorb more archers in a given area, as the lethal danger of their armament drops to practically zero beyond a hundred yards or so. In brushy cover, it may be markedly less. On the theme of bow safety, California recently quizzed the game departments of all other states and found that three had recorded instances of hunters being struck by stray arrows. Only two states reported fatalities, one of which was an archer who tripped and fell on a broadhead.

The same survey revealed that records of game lost after being hit by archers were just as favorable. Deer loss estimates did not exceed 5 per cent of the animals hit, which is considerably below losses estimated for gun-shot deer.

Special archery seasons and bow-hunting preserves, now common throughout the states, contribute their bit to the conservation aspects of the sport. Their effect is to provide additional days afield for the sportsman, leveling off the peak pressures on wildlife. Archery license fees enlarge funds badly needed to step up game management programs.

Archers play a useful role in managing deer herds on many state and national wildlife refuges. At 40,000-acre Necedah Refuge in north-central Wisconsin, for example, the area's prime aim is to shelter 75,000 migratory geese and ducks. Deer thrive there too, but at times threaten to overpopulate the feeding facilities. As a solution, archers were long ago suggested as being less bothersome to the birds than gunning operations; thus, they're invited annually to help harvest the surplus deer.

Bringing down the fleet-footed gamester with the royal rack of antlers seems always to have been the most cherished prize of the hunting archer. It remains the supreme test of archery skill.

Game management officials are not concerned about bow hunters annihilating the national deer herd. In my own state of Pennsylvania, for instance, bow hunters pursuing the wily white-tail numbered over 76,000 in 1960, highest for the nation. We bagged 1,409 of the critters, meaning that more than 98 out of 100 of us got skunked, including yours truly! The Minnesota season for 1959 offers an interesting comparison. There was a splendid deer herd and hunting conditions were the best. Some 200,000 gunners harvested 104,000 deer, for a success ratio of 53 per cent. Meanwhile, 12,000 archers took but 390 head, meaning that only 3.3 out of 100 bowmen scored.

The best record for archer-hunters I have seen occurred in the Montana 1959-60 deer season. Slightly more than 2,100 enthusiasts downed 420 trophies for a success score of 20 per cent. Nationally, the success ratio on deer averages between 3 and 5 per cent. Other game quarry favored by bowmen are rabbits, squirrels, bears, pigs and foxes, in about that order of popularity after deer. However, records are incomplete regarding archers' luck on these species.

Thus, it's clear that the archer plays a supporting role in regulating game numbers, one of the important aims of wildlife conservation. For the successful bow hunter, there is much effort involved in playing this role. First, there are long hours of patient practice with the weapon. Equally important, the archer must have studied his game, down to the last detail of habits, feed, cover and movements, just to get within bow-shooting range. More so than other Nimrods, the bowman is forced to become a practical conservationist at the outset.

Sportsmanship, I firmly believe, is part of the conservation atmosphere. On the bow-hunting trails, I have seen only one incident of bad conduct; it was a case of a "meat hunter" finding a fresh-killed deer, pulling out the rightful owner's arrow, and inserting his own. Otherwise, the national record supports the view that archers have blazed a bright trail in respect for the law, and in all-around good behavior afield.

In the over-all interest of conservation, it would seem that field

N. Y. Conservation Dept.

Rolland Schlict of Syracuse drags out a whitetail buck harvested with his bow. Trophy was taken during a special bow hunt authorized by the New York State Conservation Department at the Howland Island Refuge.

archery encourages intelligent use of land. Our club's 14-target course offers a good sample. Before the bow-bending members of the club took hold of the 6-acre site, it was a sadly neglected patch of brush and dilapidated second-growth timber. There was no real reason for its being, except as a buffer zone for the skeet, trap, handgun and rifle ranges. Rough, steep and jungled, it was little more than a fire hazard.

It's an entirely different picture today. Target alleyways and foot trails have been laid out on the contour levels, protecting soils from erosion. Regular snagging and spraying have controlled the rank growth of woody vegetation. Trailside spring waters have been developed for thirsty bowmen and wildlife. There is greatly improved access for brush fire control. And, finally, the area is both used and appreciated, after long years of virtual abandonment.

In similar ways, thousands of field-archery courses now scattered around the U. S. A. are extracting recreational advantages from the many odd areas, while at the same time protecting resources they contain.

I recently asked a number of state game and fish department directors to forward their honest opinions of archers as related to progress in better hunting conditions and administration.

Replies represented Florida, California, Minnesota, Montana, Alaska, Oklahoma, Pennsylvania and Arizona, which I took to be a fair country-wide sampling. All were enthusiastic on the influence of bowmen afield — and optimistic about the future. Commented our Florida correspondent: "As a general rule, we encourage archery as a form of outdoor recreation that may be enjoyed year round, rather than being limited just to the hunting season." Added Pennsylvania: "We feel that the opportunity to hunt with bow and arrow has provided thousands of persons a great number of additional hours afield, without adversely affecting game populations in our Commonwealth."

In a nutshell, one might say, "Archery *is* good conservation."

XIV

Safe Shooting

The sight of a broadhead arrow shearing completely through the rib cage of a white-tailed deer is an awe-inspiring lesson. The trouble is, too few people have witnessed an educational spectacle of this type. And so, we have the annual crop of accidents that could have been avoided if the following principles were observed:

1. Respect the bow for what it is. It is an instrument that can kill, inflict serious injury, or cause grave damage to property.
2. Never aim or draw an arrow in the direction of any object or target you do not fully intend to hit.
3. Shooting an arrow straight up is a stupid invitation to have it fall straight down on you or one of your friends.
4. Lay out target lanes in a manner to avoid cross fire from archers shooting at neighboring targets.
5. When searching for miss-arrows, have someone stand at the target to signal "hold fire"; or lay your bow across the target face.
6. Carry sharp broadheads with extreme caution to protect

yourself and your hunting companions. For example, when crossing fences and walls, put the broadheads over first; then, you follow.

7. Examine your bow, arrow and string carefully before shooting. Defects that give way without warning can have explosive consequences.

8. Hold your face well out of potential harm's way whenever you brace your bow, lest the bow slip and recoil.

Among shooting sports, archery has enjoyed a splendid reputation for safety. All of us, as responsible citizens of the archers' world, can work to keep it that way.

Statue of Robin Hood at Nottingham Castle excites the imagination of an English youngster. Tales of the Sherwood Forest outlaw have stirred archery enthusiasts around the world.

British Travel Assn.

XV

Signs That Point to Happy Hunting

Comes a time of year when bowmen tire of punishing the practice bales, braided grass mats and paper faces with concentric rings printed thereon. The primitive urge to test their skills and wits on the fleet, smart, furred and feathered creatures of forest and field develops a nagging strength.

Splendid exercise and long hours of reflection on the beauties of nature are rewarding, even though game bags are empty at the end of the trail. For the man who desires mightily to score, there may be a lingering sense of frustration. The archer who has not learned to pick a precise mark — not just a general area — and hit it, will be distracted to find no bull's-eye painted on the game.

Then, too, the quarry's outlines are hazy against leafy backgrounds. Shooting lanes are not clear-cut. Nor will the rascals stay still; they're off in flight at the twang of the bowstring. The arrow finds only a vacuum.

Field marksmanship "for keeps" will come with patient practice and experience. But the meager take for most bow hunters, I am sure, continues as long as they fail to "read" the landscape properly. With a moderate amount of study and observation, the archer can readily learn where to look for various species.

More than 80 per cent of all hunting sorties take place on the nation's farm and ranch lands. Although gunners are increasingly restricted by the "posting" of private property, bowmen are as yet having a little less difficulty with landowners.

Therefore, I can offer no better advice to bow hunters than to befriend farmers or ranchers. Organized bow sportsmen can accomplish this handily. There are any number of projects such as tree planting, brush fire prevention, and marshland development, wherein farmer-sportsmen co-operation pays off in mutual benefits. The farmer gains improvement for his land and water resources; meanwhile, the hunter demonstrates his worthiness of the right to hunt.

The modern farm or ranch is an ideal setting for bow sport. It offers clear shooting lanes, favorable stands and, often, abundant targets. For today's enlightened dairyman, stockman or cash cropper is also, in effect, a game manager who is well aware of wildlife values. Farming operations in many sections of the country have encouraged and multiplied game populations to heights never known even by the early Indians and white settlers.

True it is that the real big fellows such as the moose, elk, buffalo, wolf, and cougar have had to give way. On the other hand, deer and many of the smaller game such as rabbits, quail, squirrels, European partridges, raccoons, and ring-necked pheasants flourish often as by-products of conservation farming methods.

Game signs on well-managed farmland loom as big as billboards, once you have learned to recognize them. They appear as a dozen or more conservation practices installed especially to attract game; or in the form of a larger number of crop-conserving measures, which indirectly improve game habitat. Here are a few general guidelines to follow with your favorite hunting bow in hand:

When you are hunting crop fields, look for long, narrow strips of brushy or grassy cover. If you spot them, chances are strong

USDA-SCS

Knowledge of conservation helps hunting. Border of lespedeza and autumn olive is a good spot to look for bunnies, pheasants and other small game.

they're travel lanes for pheasants, doves, rabbits, and quail, leading to food and water supplies.

In grasslands, note that mowing and grazing reduces both food *and* cover. Therefore, look for planted strips and block areas where tall growth provides these game essentials.

Where cover is ample, as in farm woodlands and brushy areas, long strips of food plants are the hunter's "sign." The landowner realized that dense shade blanks out the natural food growths. He added a home-grown "cafeteria" for the wildlife.

Now, we'll get more specific:

Game Cover Strips for Croplands

Living fences of multiflora rose, field windbreaks, shrubby hedgerows, ditch banks and headlands seeded to grass and legumes, and stream-bank plantings — these are the signs you'll find in croplands. The long cover strips are superhighways. Pheasants, quail and cottontails travel them to widespread nesting places on the farm. So do prairie chickens and sharp-tail grouse on their way to banquets of waste grain and weed seeds.

There's game food in many conservation plants — the rose, privet, dogwoods, lespedezas, clovers and several grasses — but that's not their main purpose. Look there for game hiding or traveling under cover.

In windbreaks, even the squirrel hunter may find a target. Fox squirrels use them as avenues of invasion.

Favorite wintering grounds for pheasants, grouse, and rabbits are willow plantations along streams. They're an ideal screen, too, for the duck hunter who likes jump shooting.

Food and Cover Blocks for Grasslands

Look sharp for food and cover developments around ponds, near meadows, pastures and rangeland — also near marshes and similar odd areas. Nearly two million ponds have been built in American soil conservation districts. Most of them attract waterfowl, and many in the North and West produce broods of ducks. When fenced and planted, they hold added promise for the dove hunter and sharpshooter after western quail.

In the East, state game agencies help farmers establish small marshes for waterfowl. Also, they improve natural marshes with water controls and food plantings. The marshes produce ducks, furbearers and wintering areas for pheasants.

Odd areas — eroding, steep, rocky land, and hard-to-reach corners — are the usual acreage that farmers and ranchers devote to game production. Commonest measures are to protect such spots from fire and to fence livestock out. Sometimes worthless trees are removed to coax along natural food and cover. Often, landowners seed in patches of grasses, clovers or lespedezas, or plant to shrubs.

Mercury Sportsphotos

Sharpshooters all, these Pennsylvania bowmen each bagged a pheasant the first day of the season, taking full advantage of the Keystone State's conservation farm game program.

Food Strips in Woods

The hunter of ruffed grouse and deer can also follow "signs" of the farmer's activities in behalf of his sport. There's good stalking where food growths are actually planted, or encouraged by cutting back trees, along the edges of woods. In the Southeast, shrub lespedezas — high-class quail food — occur in borders, or in strips through open woodland. Elsewhere, dogwoods, autumn olive and other fruit-bearing plants are established; or farmers

Florida Game & Fish Comm.

Rough platform in pine tree gives Florida archer a vantage point for shooting deer.

will seed strips of millet, corn, sorghum, soybeans, cowpeas and hay-type lespedezas.

Where Eastern farmers cut back edges of woods, the natural growth of blackberries, cherries, grapes, thorn apples and dogwoods are choice locations for ruffed grouse, deer and rabbits.

More Signs for the Hunter

Other farm and ranch measures can guide the bowman. They are not especially designed for wildlife, but they do benefit game in important ways.

A system of using croplands for conservation, called strip-cropping, furnishes mile after mile of excellent pheasant cover. Nothing suits the pheasant hunter better than strips of corn or small grains to hunt in. Strip-cropping — always on the contour level of the land or crosswise to the prevailing wind — is one of the most common signs and easiest to see.

Grassed waterways, designed to remove water safely from the slopes, are a sign of good nesting places for quail, pheasants and cottontails. Their special wildlife value is that farmers do not mow them until after the nesting season.

A fence around the farm woodland to keep livestock out is a good notice for the gray squirrel hunter. The bushy-tails are seldom found where woods are heavily grazed.

Knee-high or taller grasses on the open range are a sign the rancher is a conservationist. Look here for prairie chickens and scaled quail, too, in improved rangelands. In Texas, you'll find white-winged doves feasting on the seeds of high-grade range grass.

Waterfowlers find irrigation reservoirs on farms in the Mississippi Flyway and in the coastal areas a sign of top-quality hunting. These reservoirs, large and shallow, are on the increase in U. S. farmland everywhere.

Thus, the signs are there for the bow hunter to see, if he will but look. Of course, there is a great deal more involved in bringing home the bacon than sharpshooting and knowing where game is likely to be found. The serious hunter will be rewarded by studying all authentic information on each species' habits of movement and reaction, daily and throughout the open season. Known patterns of feeding, resting, fighting and even playing will better prepare the bowman for what to expect.

And just as you've become *certain* of what to expect — the critters will do exactly the opposite. Yes, happily, there are rugged individuals among wildlife, too!

XVI

On the Go – With a Bow

Ever-widening opportunities to hunt and fish with the bow induce archers to "hit the trail," the year around. On land or water, there is a rich and sporty variety of live targets.

For the hunter, most states have legalized bow-taking of a dozen or more protected small game species, several types of big game, and a half dozen or so kinds of fur-bearer.

In between game seasons each state permits an arm-long list of varmints, predators and other unprotected species to entice the archer afield. And, if this were not enough, laws frequently afford the bow hunter up to an *extra month* of big game sport — in advance of gunning periods. During early, special seasons, the game trails often belong to bowmen only. Always check the law before hunting.

Those accustomed to the hue and cry of firearms hunting may be amazed by the contrasting atmosphere when bowmen take the field. One listens in vain for echoing gunfire; signal shouts; boots crashing through brush; car doors slamming, and engines snarling as gunners hustle from one covert to another.

Quietly, thoroughly and slowly the successful bowman hunts. He must get close. He hopes for a standing, sitting or slowly moving target. He prays for an unobstructed lane to shoot through. He implores the gods of the chase to give him, finally, a position where he can freely aim, draw and shoot his arrow, before the quarry is aroused and scared into the next county. The odds are by far in favor of the game.

Archers and gunners alike profit from studying the traditional lore of hunting. Quick identification of game species, ability to anticipate their movements, recognition of productive areas, all these pay off. So do other aspects of hunter performance: patience; attention to details; physical endurance; and the frequency of hunting sorties, or numbers of hours afield. And, of course, when the chips are down, marksmanship is the final factor.

Killing humanely and with dispatch is as much a sign of good sportsmanship among archers as with gun hunters. For that reason, most state laws prescribe use of the broadhead for big game. Experience also dictates use of the bladed head for many medium-size gamesters, such as fox, wildcat, turkey, raccoon, pig, and groundhog. Use field points, blunts, and other special heads for smaller targets such as pheasant, squirrel, rabbit, opossum, porcupine, skunk and so on.

Insuring that broadheads are razor-edged is but an extension of the sportsmanship attitude. Yet, it is overlooked too often. Filing or honing of heads, or use of one of the efficient sharpening devices, should be a number-one preliminary for any hunt.

A typical state hunting law requires that archers "use a bow capable of propelling a 1-ounce arrow a distance of 150 yards." The standard is modest. There are numerous medium-draw (35-50-pound) models on today's market capable of tossing a broadhead twice that distance. Such bows will have a swift, flat (nonlobbing) line of flight favorable to sniping in thick brush or woodland.

Amassing of sufficient kill-power leads to another thought bow hunters (and gunners) often neglect. An archer just *might* knock over a big buck and then, what to do? A man-sized, keen-edged hunting knife for bleeding, dressing and skinning; a length of rope for hoisting and dragging the carcass; sacking or other material to fend off the blowflies — all these are vital aids.

In his stalking, still-hunting manner of approach, the archer pays special heed to accessories gauged for silence and concealment. Bows may be blackened, swathed in tape, or slipped into close-fitting covers to prevent chance reflections of sunlight. Bowmen's faces and hands, too, are often darkened with make-up. Bright-hued, noisy-surfaced clothing is shunned in favor of camouflaged coveralls, or garments that blend readily into natural landscapes.

Arrows carried in back- or belt-quivers had best be muffled in sound-absorbent materials, lest their rattling send the alarm. Thus, the soundless bow quiver, holding three or four shafts ready to hand, comes into its own. So, also, do brush buttons affixed near bowstring nocks, where they prevent snagging as archers glide through low vegetation.

Twang of the bowstring, normally music to the archer's ear, becomes a nuisance in the game fields. Its sound may be dampened by one of several types of silencers applied to the string.

Bowmen who respect their quarry's ability to scent danger prepare accordingly. They douse themselves with various formulas, to neutralize human spoor, smell of automobiles, the aroma of tobacco smoke. Other compounds are tried in hopes the vapors will tantalize, charm and attract game within favorable shooting range. Artificial calls are often employed for similar purposes. Laborious as these details seem to be, many are religiously practiced by bowmen who regularly bring home a full bag.

I believe the finer points add a richness to the hunting experience, whether or not they pay off in countable spoils. Much of the joy of any sporting trip, one soon learns, arises from getting ready. Character traits of individual bowmen often show up in the nature and extent of their preparations. One of my friends, a good and thorough schoolteacher, carries his thoroughness to the deer country. On such a mission, he wouldn't even think of rolling out of his yard before spraying his entire sedan with a buck-scent mixture.

On a long day in the field, there are moments when suspense wears thin. Monotony or discomfort threatens to take over. Thereupon, forethought in bringing along a candy bar, a sandwich, a bit of fruit, or a small thermos of hot beverage will do wonders for the jaded spirit. These can be easily accommodated in a small belt pouch, or in the utility compartment featured on most back quivers.

A feather-light folding canvas stool may be just the thing to brighten the outlook at an hours-long vigil in the blind or at the still-hunting stand. In cold weather, look to thermal underpants and tiny hand warmers to head off sagging morale. Hunting with bow is a joyful sport, not an endurance contest.

The midday hours, when the sun is high and the game lies low, are those most likely to drag slowly for the hunter. My Nimrod buddy, Ed, has a remedy for this. He takes it on quests for deer. Ingredients are a slingshot and an assortment of squirrel, crow and varmint calls. When things get dull he sets up his plaintive cries. Whatever responds, Ed wings away at 'em with his quiet slinger. If deer are in the offing, they aren't disturbed. Meanwhile, Ed's got a little subsport going, and time goes merrily by.

Water-Sport Fever

Whoever dreamed up the expression, "easy as shooting fish in a barrel," was more than a little bit off the beam. It is not a cinch to zero in on fish in any body of water, as veteran bow fishermen will assure you. It would be a great deal simpler if the finny tribe would float conveniently on the surface. But they don't often do that. This poses the toughest phase of the problem.

Looked at from above, water acts as a prism. This means that submerged objects, like fish, *appear* to be where they aren't. They *look* closer to the surface than they *are*. Another little twist is that your arrow will start deflecting upwards the instant it strikes the water. It all adds up to the fact that you should aim at a spot *below* your underwater target. There are so many variables that aiming rules of thumb are meaningless. Shoot. Shoot some more, and let experience be your teacher.

Murky, weedy waters will offer further stumbling blocks, as will the blinding bounce of sunlight from certain angles of vision. To combat the latter, I would strongly recommend polarized sunglasses; they do a nice job on glare and singling out the fish.

Surfaced or partly surfaced targets offer the happiest moments. Carp will come up and roll during their late-spring to early-summer spawning season and for that reason are no doubt the most commonly bow-shot fish. In the Southland, alligator gar are brought to the surface by hook-and-line methods, and then spectacularly dispatched by archer-marksmen. Eels are bagged as they wriggle in reedy marshes or when they resort to overland traveling.

Looking seaward, there is no end of possible targets, as few legal regulations apply. Sting rays, sea turtles, red drum, mackerel, herring, tuna, marlin and many other species will often trend surfaceward when feeding, spawning or being chased by predators. I have talked with archers who have outboarded after spawning sharks in shallow, tidal estuaries; riddled them with arrows; and actually boated a few of the smaller man-eaters. To them I say welcome to my share of that hobby, and hats off to their adventurous spirit.

Ocean bow-fishing, it must be said, tends to mean ultralong excursions in order to locate targets. Wading, knee- to waist-deep, in search of fresh-water prey is likely to be more rewarding.

A Way to Travel

Searching out the haunts of game and fish is but one method by which archery whets the wanderlust, the overpowering yen to see the world around us. Indulging in the weekend shoots at one, another, and another of the thousands of field courses is a colorful travelogue through ever-varying landscape. Annual jaunts to national tournaments, always held amid spectacular scenery, are splendid for itchy feet.

Each year sees more special, regional attractions added to the calendar for the touring bowman. "Festivals" for archers, usually held just before the big game season, are increasingly popular events of this type. There is a county-fair atmosphere of good eats, plenteous action and vigorous sociability. Archers match skills at field courses, novelty targets, game-calling and the like, then take to the coverts for live game such as wild boar, foxes and 'coons. There are exhibits, demonstrations, movies and dances, and the inevitable queen-of-the-archers contest. There is fun for archers and onlookers alike, and expenditures are moderate.

Beginning archers are warned: the bow truly has seven-league boots!

Index

The Author

For three years, Bernhard A. Roth was the editor of *Hunting and Fishing,* a leading sportsmen's magazine. This position allowed him to write as well as hunt. In his current job as Chief Public Information Officer for the U. S. Soil Conservation Service in the Northeastern States, one of his tasks is to convince the public that nothing is more important than taking better care of America's natural wonders—her soil, water, woodlands and wildlife. This is Mr. Roth's first book for young people.